CHÂTEAU LATOUR

MICHEL DOVAZ

FOREWORD MICHAEL BROADBENT

PHOTOGRAPHS LAZIZ HAMANI

ASSOULINE

To N. L.,
patiently

© Assouline, 1998
26-28 rue Danielle Casanova
75002 Paris (France)
Tel: +33 1 42 60 33 84 Fax: +33 1 42 60 33 85
http://www.imaginet.fr/assouline

Distributed to the US trade by St. Martin's Press
Distributed in Canada by McClelland & Stewart
Distributed in all other countries by Thames and Hudson (Distributors) Ltd, London

ISBN: 2 84323 100 0

Photographs (except archival documents): Laziz Hamani
© Laziz Hamani/Editions Assouline
Photo page 173 © Duclos/Gamma

Design: Isabelle Ducat
Translated from the French by Chanterelle Translations, London © Assouline

Colour separation: Gravor (Switzerland)
Printed and bound by Christie's International Group
Printing Division (Great Britain)

CONTENTS

FOREWORD

BY

MICHAEL BROADBENT

atour: the name alone is concise, solid and dependable; as distinctive and as memorable as its ancient tower. The wine too is solid and dependable, not in a heavy or clumsy way but packed with fruit and all the essential component parts. Though fairly tough, tannic and mouth-filling when young, the wine of Latour has the breed and balance which, supremely, enables it to develop harmoniously over a period of time.

Not only is Latour famous for its longevity, it has the almost unique, certainly uncommon, capability of producing good wine even in a poor year. For example, I well remember the 1963, 1965 and 1968 vintages, all generally execrable because of a calamitously wet, sunless, growing season; yet, thanks to a superbly drained site, rigorous selection of grapes, patient and skilful wine making, Latour, virtually alone in these three years, managed to produce surprisingly drinkable wine.

Mention of longevity reminds me of several memorable tastings of Latour which demonstrated the remarkable quality and stamina of many of the old vintages. The first Latour tasting, indeed the first major 'vertical' tasting of its type, was held in Fort Worth, Texas, in May 1976. Host was Dr. Marvin Overton, a noted neurosurgeon and connoisseur of wine, commentaries being by M. Henri Martin, then *gérant* of Latour, and myself. The tasting comprised forty-seven vintages of Latour, ranged in 'flights', young to old, the oldest being the 1899, which astonished everyone with its relative freshness and charm. Five years later, this time in San Francisco, I attended a "Fête du Château Latour" comprising no fewer than eighty-six vintages starting with 1979, the oldest of all being a pre-phylloxera 1861. The monumental 1928 had by then only just reached its plâteau of perfection — it had taken half a century to mature! It is still perfection.

entioning Americans and old vintages is a timely, if historic, reminder that Latour was a well-established *premier cru* long before the official classification of the wines of the Médoc in 1855, for, as related by Nicholas Faith in his book *Latour* (Christie's Wine Publications, London, 1991), Thomas Jefferson, following his visit to Bordeaux in May 1787, reported in a letter to a friend that there were "four first growths", of which M. Miromesnil's "La Tour de Ségur" (Latour) was one. Jefferson, then American 'envoy' in Paris was a noted connoisseur, a man of wide interests and enquiring mind: he visited all the top châteaux, ordering wine on the spot and insisting, incidentally, on château bottling! On his return to Philadelphia he wrote in 1791 to various château proprietors via his agent in Bordeaux to order further supplies of wine for himself and the President, George Washington. For example "to the Count Miromenil [sic] of Ségur" requesting "20 dozen bottles of your best wine for drinking now, packed and marked 'G.W.' at the vineyard". Alas, Latour could not supply, Miromesnil's *homme d'affaire* informing him that "he had no wine on hand that could do justice to the estate". In retrospect, it is a pity that Jefferson did not return to his post in Paris, for had he done so he might have crossed La Manche to London to bid for "a case" containing "50 quart bottles of the growths of Latour and vintage 1785" offered for sale by Mr. James Christie on 1 August 1792. (A standard 'case' at that time was a large wicker box or 'hamper', and a 'quart' was the normal size Bordeaux bottle but with a more slender shoulder and neck.) This, as a matter of interest, was the first mention of Latour in a London auction catalogue though 'claret', the peculiarly English generic term for red Bordeaux, had featured regularly at auction

since Mr. Christie's first sale, for a "Nobleman deceas'd" in December 1766. Two centuries later, Christie's opened a new specialist wine department under my management, Latour making a welcome reappearance at the first of the new season of wine sales in the auction of 1966.

Just over a decade later, in June 1977, we were privileged to mount "An Important Sale of Grand Vin de Château Latour", the illustrated catalogue listing eighty-two vintages, including every vintage from 1976 back to 1916 (Latour did not make any wine in 1915) and older wines, ending up with the 1863. The 'star' lot was an *Impériale* of the magnificent 1900 which sold for £2800, a very high price at that time.

ut, enough about history and close links with Christie's. What about the wine? And how is the present team coping? Happily, well, for I have noticed that those who work for companies with a high reputation have a strong incentive to live up to that reputation which is, of course, based on quality: quality of the product and quality of service.

In the case of a *premier cru* vignoble, the foundation or ground base is, almost literally, the *terroir*, which in this instance relates not just to soil and subsoil but to drainage, aspect and microclimate. Also implicit is the selection of suitable vine stocks and the all-important 'husbandry', viticulture. Then follows the skilled technical work necessary for the conversion of ripe grapes into fine wine, finally its *élevage*.

It is so easy to pull a cork, to taste, to drink, to criticise. It is quite another thing to create, to turn an agricultural product into a work of art. This requires experience and expertise. Some châteaux, even of *premier cru* status, have had their ups and downs. What is so noticeable about Latour is its consistency and typicity, making the best in often unpredictable and difficult weather conditions and meeting the demands of the market.

The market is a vital factor, for without the customer, via the trade, being willing and able to pay a substantial price, fine wine will not be made. Happily the age-old reliance on a relatively few, often aristocratic, connoisseurs, the upper-class élite, has been augmented and to an extent superseded by enthusiastic and knowledgeable 'wine buffs' worldwide. The great wines of Bordeaux are now appreciated by those with the wealth and leisure to appreciate the best. It is now a truly global market.

This new book, featuring one of the greatest of all red Bordeaux, is therefore timely. Happily, Michel Dovaz, an old friend whose knowledge and understanding of wine I have always respected, does full justice to the subject; to Latour, its châteaux and in particular its wine, which is so greatly admired by the new international brotherhood of wine.

MICHAEL BROADBENT

Christie's, London

FROM THE
CO-SEIGNEURIE TO SOLE OWNERSHIP
OR THE TRIUMPH OF WILL

xtraordinary wines have an extraordinary history. Everyone has heard of Château Latour as a fine wine, the first *cru* (growth) classified in 1855. But the history of the *domaine* is less well-known; that of the origins of the Latour wine, those who created it or the generations who continued to make it down the generations.

Latour owes its existence to one family, the Mullet family. First there was Arnaud de Mullet, who amassed land in the sixteenth century which he turned into a noble estate or *seigneurie*. The first Denis de Mullet, his son, who succeeded him, turned the lands into a wine-producing *domaine*. This is how the daughter of Denis, Catherine de Mullet, might have told the story of Latour to her son:

"My son, when I married your father, many years ago in 1621, like all wives, I had to leave my family. I was no longer a de Mullet, but instead became a Daulède. My father lived to a great age, as his father did before him; it could even be said that old age was a tradition in our family. Unfortunately, this tradition seems to have been lost. I would go further and say that the de Mullet family seems doomed to die young. My brother, Gabriel, who, like his grandfather, Arnaud, had a brilliant career as a privy counsellor in the King's parliament, the high judicial court, died five years after his marriage in 1639. So he died even before your father, who outlived him by twelve years. That is why Gabriel's son, the second Denis, inherited the Latour title and estates when he was not yet fifteen years of age. It was my sister-in-law, Jehanne de Pontcastel, who managed her son's estate, the Latour *seigneurie*.

"Alas! The premature demise of my nephew, in March 1660, ended the direct male line of descent from Arnaud de Mullet. What was more serious, his death seemed to make a mockery of the slow and laborious effort which had been invested in acquiring and building up the Latour estate.

Opposite: The Château Latour emblem on the paper which is used to wrap each individual bottle of Grand Vin.

"The property, the pride of the Mullets for over a century, has now become mine through inheritance, and soon it will be yours. Although my blood, that of the Mullets, runs through your veins, I have not forgotten that you are a Daulède.

"The reason I am speaking of this now is in the hope that it will help you to understand your heritage, whose value as a family tradition is far greater than its monetary value. Every day, one sees inherited estates disappear, broken up and sold at auction by a bevy of heirs. As the sole owner of Latour, do you not run the same risk of underestimating its importance?

"The properties of the Daulède family are so numerous, you may not have the urge to devote yourself to the Latour estate, which may involve certain duties but is nevertheless a profitable concern. It is said that you plan to succeed your father-in-law, Monsieur de Montiac, as chief justice of parliament. I encourage you to do so because our two families, three if one counts the family of Thérèse, your wife, have always served our beautiful city of Bordeaux.

"These ambitions do not absolve you of the task of administering your own affairs. I should like to encourage you to take a greater interest in the Saint-Maubert land and — why conceal it? — to instil love of this family property in you, to give you an idea of its history which dates back well beyond your great-grandfather Arnaud de Mullet, who was a man of great merit.

"I shall simplify as much as I can a glorious exploit, the like of which will be sought in vain among other noble estates. I refer to the siege of 1378. The estate of Saint-Maubert or Saint-Mambert — one should say Saint-Mamert, because when our parish was created in the seventh century the intention was to honour this saint — can pride itself on its military record.

"The extremely powerful, rich and illustrious de Castillon family held the fiefdom of Saint-Mambert. In the early fourteenth century, Gaucelme de Castillon built a stronghold in his fiefdom. As a result of marriages, unfortunate inheritances and various lawsuits, the estate subsequently passed to the Bourg-Charente, Albret, and then to the Montferrand families.

"During the Hundred Years' War, Bertrand II de Montferrand became the lord of Saint-Mambert. The stronghold, fortress or "Tower", became the prize in a battle which is described in detail by Jean Froissart in the second volume of his famous *Chronicles*.

"First, the Tower was occupied by the Bretons, under the command of Captain Virelion.

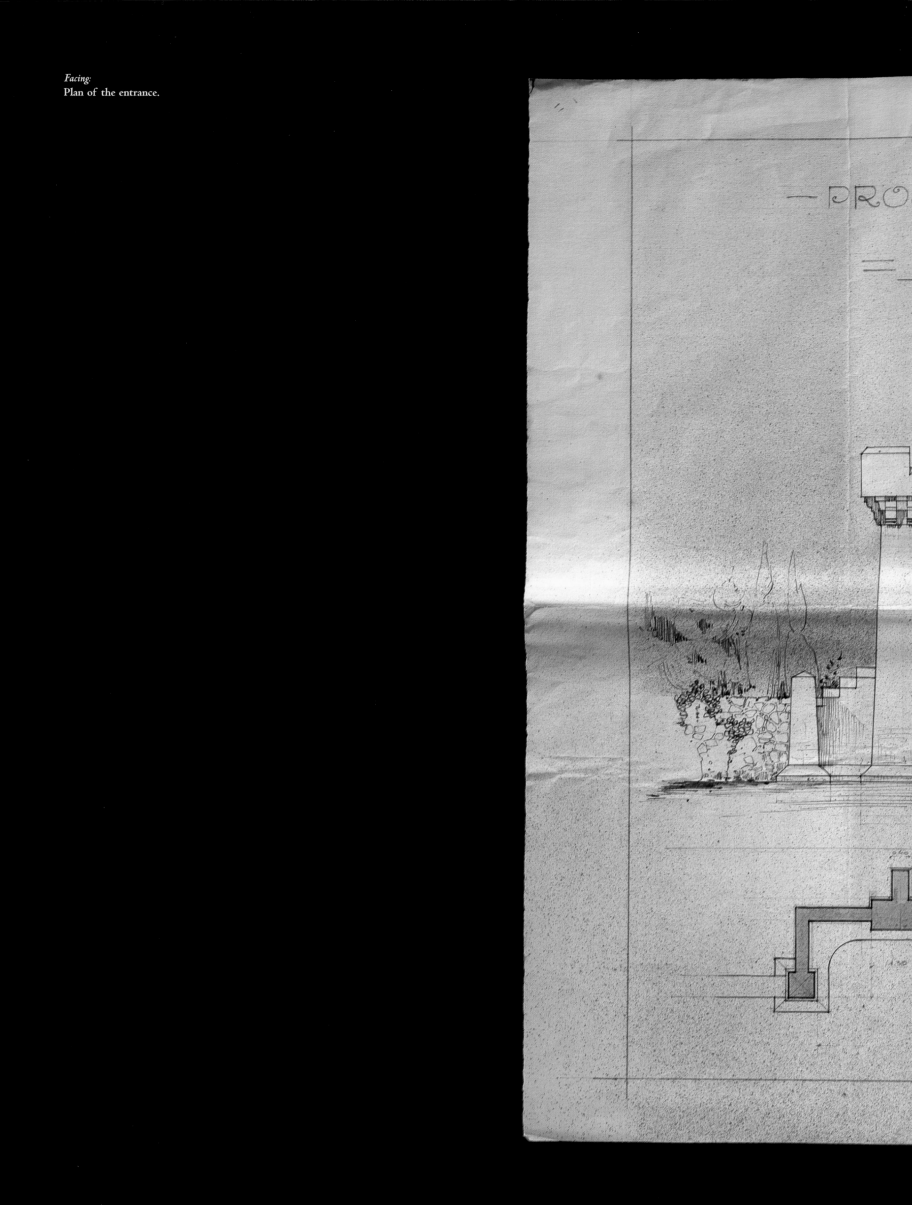

ET - D' ENTRÉE - PRINCIPALE —

DU DOMAINE

CHATEAU == LATOUR ==

FACADE sur ROUTE

COUPE

— Éch: 2 cm p/m —

CHATEAU LATOUR

0.70

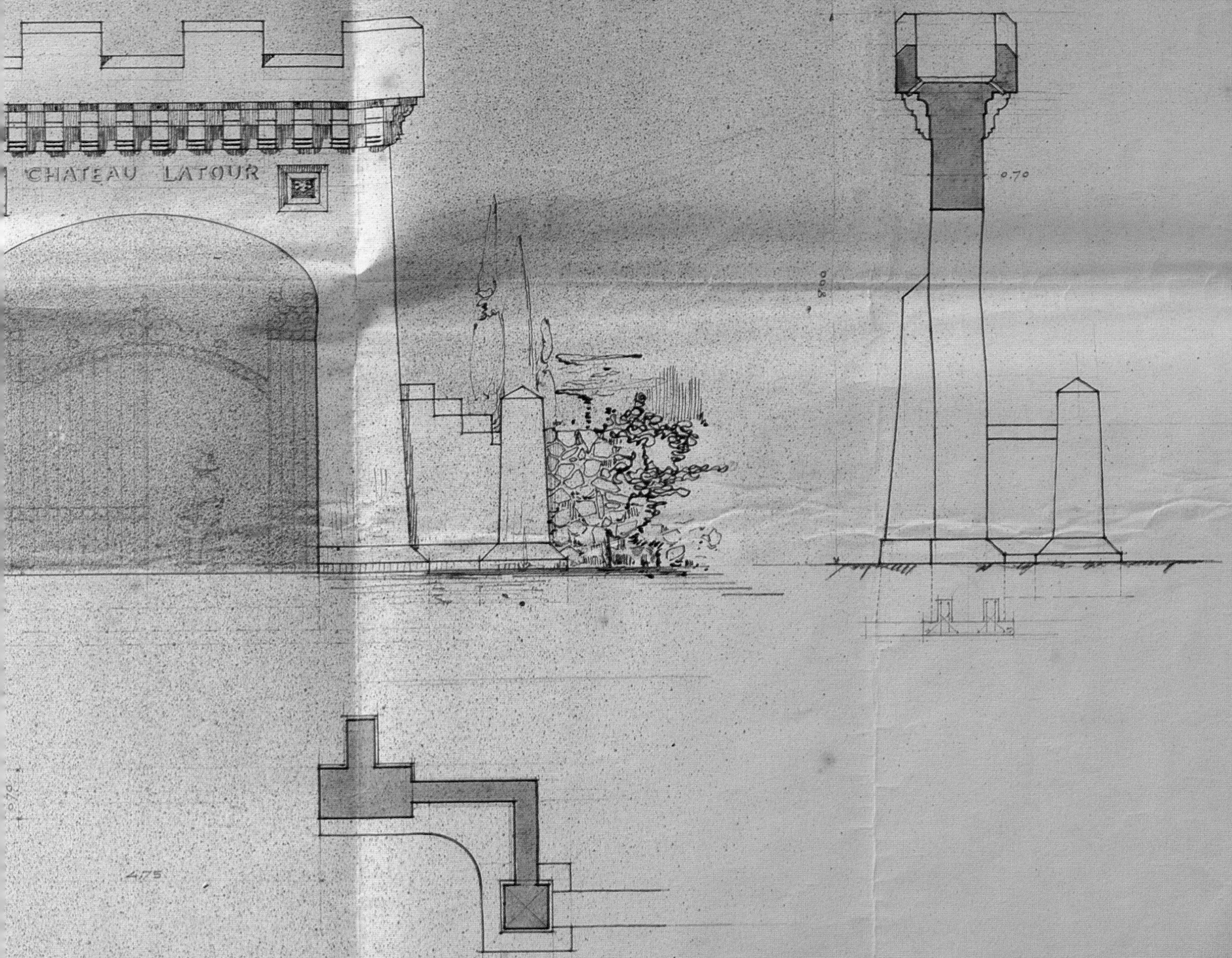

The English could not allow this pocket of French occupation to remain right in the heart of the Médoc. They decided to lay siege to Saint-Mambert (Froissart called it "Saint-Maubiert"). Three hundred lancers led the first assault but made little progress. The next day, the artillery was let loose in the form of catapult engines and mangonels, to make the roofs of the tower they were in collapse.

"On the third day, the Bretons parlayed. The Tower was later repaired and was defended by a garrison. It is said that the Tower was besieged yet again on 18 July 1453, the day after the Battle of Castillon, but that has never been corroborated. At the end of the Hundred Years' War, the Albret family were granted the Tower, before being dispossessed of it by three nobles – Gaston de l'Isle, Marguerite Treulo and Saint-Genès.

"The Tower, known simply as 'La Tour', ceased to be a fortification. Henceforward, the estate was jointly owned as a *co-seigneurie*. After a buyout, the de l'Isle and Saint-Genès families shared the estate between them.

"It was at this point that your great-grandfather, Arnaud de Mullet, counsellor then president of the parliamentary committee of inquiry at Bordeaux, who had an eye on some land in the Médoc, especially at Saint-Laurent, bought the de l'Isle family's share of the Tower estate.

*he tenant-farmers lacked resources and land and were unable to grow the crops which were best for the particular type of soil on their plots. Not all soil is of the same richness and it is wrong to plant wheat in a field more suited to grape-growing, and vice versa.*

"I have here the original contract which specifies clearly that your grandfather should benefit, from 8 May 1571, the date of signature, from all these 'goods, quit-rents, rents, dues, fees, spoils and right of prelacy' belonging to the estates of la Tour and the Salle de Poujaux. For this, he had to pay 1100 ecus. I can tell you the price because it is written on the deed but I hope I can demonstrate to you that it was not merely a matter of acquiring power or honours, or of making a financial investment in the hope of being able to pocket the proceeds. For twenty years or more, Arnaud de Mullet purchased various fiefdoms, leases, quit-rents, tenancies, etc., between Saint-Laurent and Pauillac, until Sainxe de Saint-Genès was willing to assign him some of his rights in the La Tour estate, and Sainxe's heirs transferred to him those which they still owned in 1595. The Mullets – I say the Mullets because Arnaud had assigned part of his estate to Denis, my father, who at the time was advocate-general of the parliament –, the Mullets, as I was saying, became the sole lords of the la Tour estate.

Opposite: This is how the grapes were once harvested. Entrance to the winery.

he creation of an estate devoted to the production of the finest wines is an idea which developed in the Bordeaux region from the first half of the seventeenth century.

"This perseverance illustrates the obstinacy of the Mullets. My father bought another fiefdom bordering on Saint-Julien and Saint-Mambert and, most importantly, repurchased Bourdieu de la Tour. In the early days, he had a list drawn up of his land in order to be able to be sure to draw rents from all of it. This inventory served him for the last fifteen years of his life, when he bought out the leases on some of the properties in order to create an estate which he farmed directly, or rather through an estate manager who lived there and was paid for this work. The purchases were time-consuming and numerous. It is true that several tenant-farmers whose arrears had been allowed to grow indefinitely, did not earn much, if anything, from the deals.

"You wish to know the point of these purchases, this expenditure, given that these tenant-farmers managed their land themselves and normally paid rent? My father realised that the tenant-farmers lacked resources and land and were unable to grow the crops which were best for the particular type of soil on their plots. Not all growing soil is of the same rich-ness and it is wrong to plant wheat in a field more suited to grape-growing, and vice versa.

"The quality of Saint-Mambert wine had long been recognised. Jean de Treulo, a wine merchant, who was already dealing with England in the late fourteenth century, had entered into a contract with Amadieu de la Motte, and the latter had promised to deliver to him wine only from the la Tour estate, to the exclusion of all other. In any case, you

Above: View of the Gironde estuary from the estate.

know all that you need to know about wine since your land in Margaux is covered in vines and your father-in-law, Monsieur de Pontac — as I have recently been told — is in the process of building a fortune on his new Haut-Brion claret.

"My son, I shall end this account here, as it is already too long. I have paid homage to my grandfather and my father. I hope that, despite all your preoccupations, you will ensure that all this family property enjoys a long and glorious destiny. Once you understand its worth, that alone ought to encourage you to cherish it."

But it was in vain that Madame Daulède, née Catherine de Mullet, sought to instil enthusiasm for the la Tour estate in her son Jean-Denis; on 29 June 1670 he sold it to François Chanevas.

Just over a century later, the French Revolution abolished the privileges of the nobility, but this measure had no effect on the life of the great wines, whose quality did not depend on the prerogatives of the aristocracy. The acquisition of what had once been noble estates confirmed the social position of the newly enriched middle classes but the invention and development of the *grands crus* was based mainly on economic motives.

*here are many parts of Médoc whose wines have an excellent reputation and sell well, especially Latour, Lafite and Margaux. A bill dated 1714 shows that Latour was the most expensive wine in Médoc, more costly than either Lafite or Margaux.*

The great wines established their reputation in the eighteenth century, but the importance of the previous century should not be overlooked for two good reasons: firstly it was the era in which the structure of the great estates was changed, but above all it was then that the great wines were "invented" and each *cru* acquired its own characteristics. In the seventeenth century, land in France was still worked according to the customs established in the Middle Ages. For instance, the nobility had very little control over the farmland they owned. The lord of the manor only benefited directly from poor or untillable soil while the rest of the land was worked by tenant-farmers, known as *tenanciers,* who rented it in perpetuity and whose rights — with the exception of the right to dispose of the terrain — were similar to our modern idea of ownership. Each plot of land being thus assigned, the land tenure was clearly defined by "tenants and boundaries" and was listed in the inventory of the property of the estate, known as the *terrier.* In practice, these tenancies meant that good arable land was completely outside the control of the lord of the manor. Of course, the tenant farmer had to pay rent to the landlord, the amount of which was fixed by complicated and rather quaint rules. Apart from the quit-rent, which was a

Signé avecq le Sieur procureur constitué ledit R. L.

Ministre et maytet non les autres tenanciers pour ne

sçavoir de ce jnterpellez suivant l'ordonnance, =

L'original est controllé et lesparre par courault &

Minniette   Nre Royale

Du vingt sixiéme
de Novembre mil sept cent quinze

Laqu[e] L'ardeuant moy nore Royal

En guienne soussigné present les temoins bas nommés
ont été present Jean Roux maitre masson, =

s/L'art.   Sieur Bertrand gendre maitre chirurgien, —
650.
Marguerite Larieu veuve de Sabien Drithon

& Pierre Lagune tinsran faisant comme
mary de Marie Denise habitand du bourg et parroisse
St Laurent en medoc lesquelx de leur bon gré et
vollonté pour eux et les leurs à L'auenir ont reconneu
et confessé, et par ces presentes reconnoissent et
confessent auoir et tenir en fief et coment et feodallmt
suiuant les b7 foix et coutumes de Bordeaux et
present païs de bourdelloix aux droits et deuoirs
cy apres declarés et specifiés dr mesire allexand

Segur Chevallier con.er du Roy en ses con.els

...resident amortier au parlement de Bordeaux ...

...neur de france, Lafite, Latour s.t Lambert et fief

...ppendance habitant dud bordeaux pavroisse ...

...aulin au nom et comme mary de Dame Marie

...eze de Clauzel son epouse absent, mais Sieur

...al Espaignet agent de ses affaires en sadite

...son et seigneurie de latour, et y demeurant

...roisse saint Lambert audit medoc a ce present

...v ledit seigneur et les siens a lavenir stipullant

...cceptant en consequence de la procuration ...

...esse quil en a dudit seigneur, laquelle nous

...itte apparoir en datte du vingt septieme de may

...l sept cent douze receue par Raymond no.re Royal

..auoir Est quarante quatre boutte de roguieu de

..e vigne a prendre la longueur de quarente cinq ...

...e du bout du nord dicelles, sittuées au lieu appellé

...ajellet pavroisse dudit saint Laurent, tenue a

...endre par le cotté du couchant de ladpiece tirant

...leuant tout de suitte quinse roguieu par ledit ...

..oux, sept roguieu par ledit Laguire, encore sept

...guieu par ledit roux, sept roguieu par ladite ...

...uue de Drichon, et huict roguieu par ledit sieur

...endre, Reuenant audit nombre, confrontant par

...tier du cotté dubeuant a la vigne du sieur

Facing:
**An entry dating
from 1715 in the
Latour archives.**

lump sum, he had to pay an agricultural rent, the amount of which was index-linked to yield, which varies enormously in agriculture. The dues might amount to 20 per cent of the value of the harvest, or even more; they were paid according to terms fixed by contract, like other dues. Since the lords of the manor drew their income from a number of scattered tenancies, they frequently employed agents who collected the rents and quit-rents on their behalf and took a commission. There was another type of special payment called the *esporle* or spoil, or even *esporle à double mouvance*, which had to be paid on each tenure on the death of a landlord or a tenant. This shows what a clever strategy Denis de Mullet employed to acquire the la Tour estate, in the early seventeenth century. He managed to break the tenure system and buy out the tenants' leases so as to enhance the value of the *seigneurie* as an estate to be farmed by the owners.

The creation of a *domaine* which specialised in producing great wines is an idea which started to spread through the Bordeaux region in the first half of the seventeenth century. It was at this time that the Pontac family developed their Haut-Brion vineyard. They were ahead of their time and were very directly involved. Arnaud de Pontac even sent his own son to London to sell his wine there in a tavern-cum-grocery he had established for the purpose.

*he great wines established their reputation in the eighteenth century, but the importance of the previous century should not be overlooked: firstly it was in this era that the structure of the great estates was changed, but above all it was then that the notion of great wines was "invented".*

Denis de Mullet was familiar with the wines of Margaux and Pontac Haut-Brion, since in 1621 his daughter Catherine married the owner of the Margaux vines (the future Château Margaux); furthermore, in 1654 his grandson married Thérèse de Pontac, daughter of the owner of Haut-Brion.

The wealthy families of the Bordeaux region needed much discernment in order to be able to establish estates solely devoted to the monoculture of the grape vine. The quality of the soil was a crucial factor in choosing and consolidating the land.

In the case of the la Tour estate, the land tenures covered the villages of Saint-Laurent, Saint-Lambert and Saint-Julien, and even encroached upon Pauillac. However, Denis de Mullet concentrated his efforts upon the section at Bourdieu de la Tour, and thus contributed to making the distinction between the "bourgeois" vineyard and that of the peasant.

In 1634, Denis de Mullet hired Guilhem Rousseau to tend his vines, make the wine, sow wheat, and so on. The deed was signed by Jehan Castaignet, Denis de Mullet's agent, which proved the existence of an estate and of its management.

Opposite: View of the Gironde at sunset.

In 1638, there is the first mention of a wine sold directly by la Tour. It was sent to Bordeaux by boat, having been ordered by a tavern; this transaction was no doubt arranged by Denis de Mullet using his privileged position as a leading member of the Bordeaux bourgeoisie. Finally, we need to consider the origin of wine appellations. When in 1647 the aldermen mentioned the price of wine, the wines themselves were only identified by the region in which they were produced. But sixteen years later, in 1663, the diarist Samuel Pepys wrote that he had drunk a special wine which he called "Haut-Brion". This was not a region but quite clearly the name of an estate, a trademark as one would later say, which designated the wine in question.

In 1698, the controller Bazin de Bezons was unfortunately very imprecise when he wrote: "There are many places in Médoc where the wines are esteemed and sell well", though we can be certain that Latour, Lafite and Margaux were among these places, because a bill of 1714 proves that the Latour wine was the most expensive in Médoc, more costly than either Lafite or Margaux.

In the middle of the seventeenth century, despite the archaic land tenure system, the Bordeaux region was a major wine producer, with the port of Bordeaux shipping up to one hundred thousand casks of wine a year. By the end of the century, mass production had actually begun in earnest and the future *premiers crus* had been identified, specially vinified and sold at a good price.

A long and glorious adventure had started.

Opposite: The château's reserve.

Contenances.

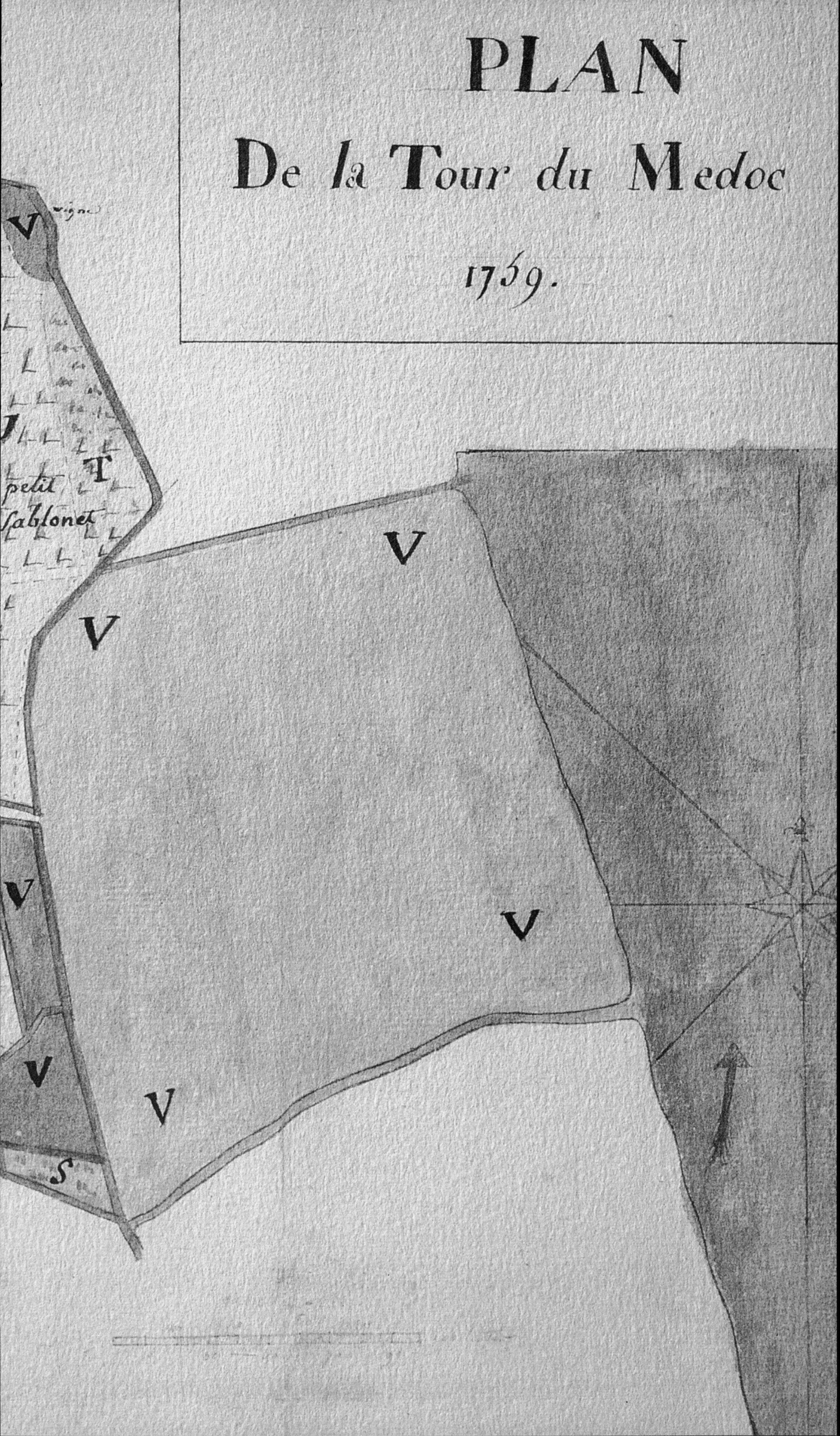

PLAN
De la Tour du Medoc

1759.

V

rigne

V

L

U

petit

sablonet

T

L L

L L

L

L

V

V

V

V

V

V

V

S

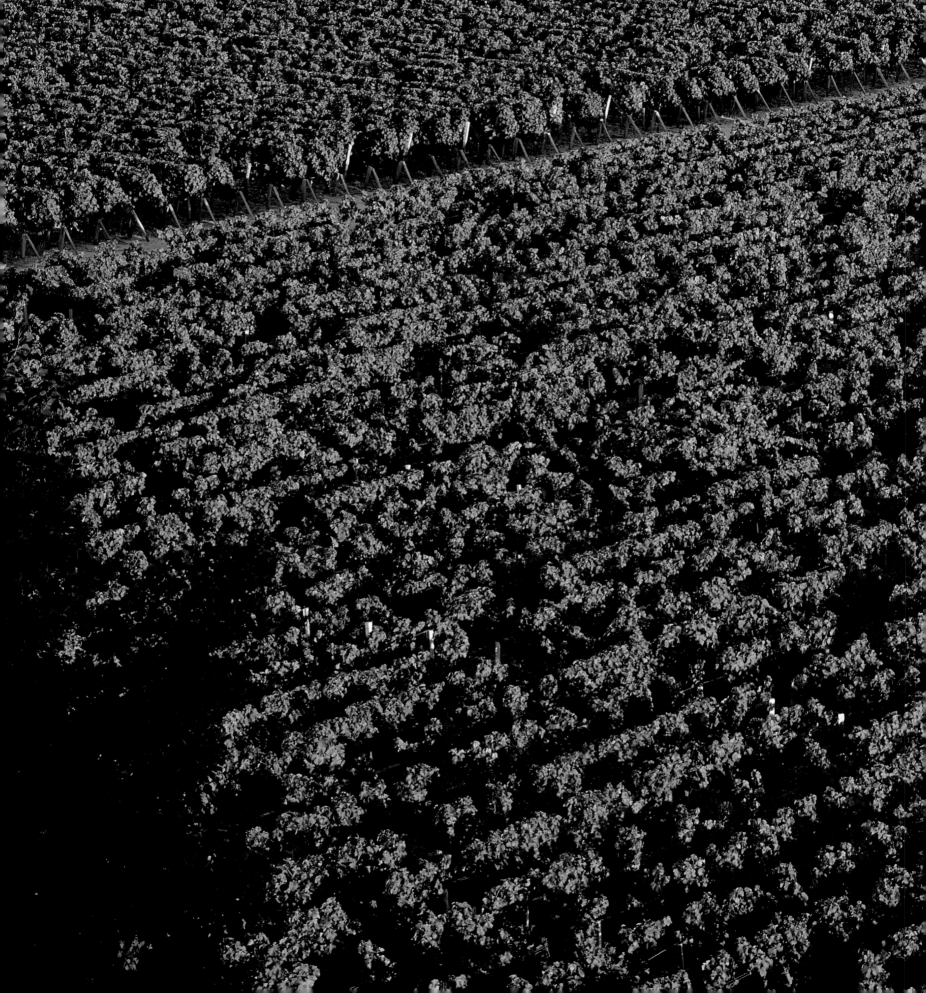

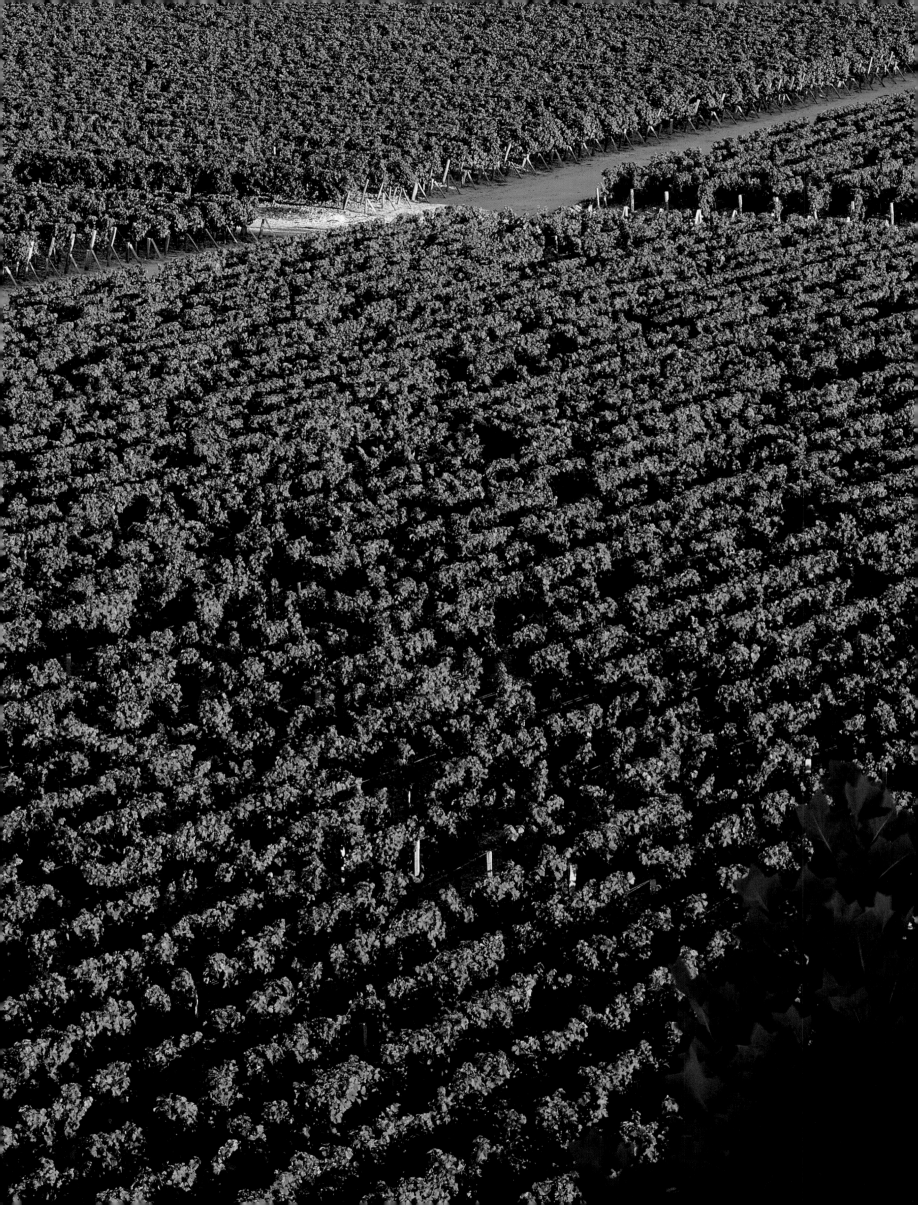

A FAMILY
TRADITION
1670-1963
OR CONTINUITY REWARDED

e have very little information about François Chanevas (or de Chanevas) to whom Jean-Denis Daulède sold the la Tour estate on 29 June 1670. He was a Parisian postmaster, who farmed out postal services and seemed to have become rich as a result. At a turning-point in his career, he settled in Bordeaux and became "Master of the Bordeaux posts and the general area of Guyenne". But this prosperity does not explain how or why, in his old age, he found 64,000 *livres tournois*, a considerable sum of money at the time, to spend on purchasing the noble house of la Tour Saint-Maubert (buildings, land, farms, rights to dispense justice), when he did not even have any direct heirs.

It is true that he devoted the interest it deserved to his new property. For example, he sued François de Foix-Candale, Baron de Lamarque, to defend his right to dispense justice over the estate of la Tour. Upon his death, the Tour Saint-Maubert went to his niece, Marguerite Coutant, who married the son of a first president of the parliament (de Nesmond), an alliance which linked the new owners of the Tower to their predecessors, who had also been prominent members of parliament. It was Marie-Thérèse, her daughter from her second marriage to Joseph de Clausel, however, who inherited the estate of la Tour upon Marguerite's death in 1693.

In 1695, Marie-Thérèse de Clausel married the rich and powerful Alexandre de Ségur, the lord of Franc, Bègles, Belfort and Saint-Ujeau. It was at this date that the estate of la Tour became part of the prosperous and extensive Ségur estate. For nearly three centuries, the successors of Alexandre de Ségur were known as "the Ségur heirs", thus perpetuating the noble lineage whose scions retained the Château Latour until 1963.

In the late seventeenth century, the fame of the estate of la Tour spread far and wide. It was

Facing:
Harvesting the grapes
in the old days.

known that it was producing a wine that was the best in the whole Médoc region, and that the vines of Médoc itself were better than any others. In fact, this first venture into wine-growing inspired Alexandre de Ségur, because soon afterwards he acquired the Lafite estate. When he died in 1716, his son, Nicolas-Alexandre, chief justice of the Bordeaux parliament, inherited Latour and Lafite, and in turn added to his property by acquiring the Mouton and Calon estates. Chief Justice Ségur's passion for the wines of Médoc do not seem to have been the result of purely financial calculations. His Lafite and Latour properties, valued at 700,000 and 500,000 *livres tournois* respectively, brought in a meagre 5 per cent profit. This was mainly the proceeds of sales to British purchasers, the only ones who really appreciated fine wines – in Northern France, wine merchants' customers were not disposed to spend large sums of money and may not have had the taste or the means to acquire these valuable vintages. So quite apart from the vagaries of the weather, the income from the great vineyards depended on the political and military climate, which sometimes placed formidable obstacles in the way of Anglo-French trade. However, the 5 per cent profit mentioned was a minimum, as studies of the royal taxation ledgers show. And the accumulation of properties by Chief Justice de Ségur clearly shows that wine-growing estates, despite being subject to serious risk, were not necessarily unprofitable.

Even if today we might find the title rather showy, there was good reason to call Nicolas-Alexandre de Ségur "the Prince of Vines", due to the extraordinary concentration in his hands of the best vineyards of Médoc. His death in 1755 caused problems for the succession, since he had left four daughters but no sons. The entire inheritance passed to the son of the eldest daughter, who had married her cousin, Alexandre de Ségur-Calon, a parliamentary counsellor; but her three younger sisters had to be compensated since they had never been awarded the dowries they had been promised.

The matter was settled by the brothers-in-law, since all four daughters had married. The eldest had married the counsellor, as has been said, and he became chief justice of Paris. Her three sisters were Angélique-Louise, Comtesse de Maisoncel, who died without issue;

Opposite: Grapes ready for harvesting.

Charlotte-Émilie, Comtesse de Coëtlogon, without issue; and finally, Marie-Antoinette Victoire, who married the Comte de Miromesnil and gave him two daughters.

The succession caused the estates amassed by Chief Justice de Ségur to be broken up. The lawsuit to settle the estate dragged on for years, and the three sisters were jointly awarded the Latour estate, then valued at just over 500,000 livres. In the next generation, the main Latour heirs were the two daughters of the Comtesse de Miromesnil, who became respectively the Comtesse de la Pallu and the Marquise de Beaumont. But a member of a collateral branch of the family named in the estate of the two other sisters, the Comte de Ségur-Cabanac, was given a quarter of the estate as his share. This was the famous *quart Latour*, which was to have mixed fortunes.

The situation was rather odd because none of the owners was born in the region, and none of them lived in Bordeaux or even nearby. The estate was thus run by estate managers, who will be introduced later, and who sometimes abused the freedom granted them by the absentee landlords.

The settlement of the succession governed life on the estate for the next two hundred years. On the one hand, there was the manor (*seigneurie*) of la Tour, which included the estate we know today, but which extended from Saint-Julien to Saint-Laurent, and the income therefrom, which never exceeded I per cent of the profits made by the wine; but above all, there was the important estate of Latour, which was cultivated directly by its owners. About twenty workers were employed permanently, and two hundred people were taken on for picking grapes at harvest time. The vines covered more than 60 acres (25 hectares), an area which was frequently extended. The 5 per cent profit made by Chief Justice Ségur was greatly exceeded, and eventually reached 12 per cent minimum.

Shortly before the French Revolution, between 1784 and 1790, the Latour profits topped the 20 per cent mark. This performance was the result of two factors, the increase in the average production of great wine, which rose from fifty casks a year in the time of Chief Justice Ségur to seventy-five casks before the Revolution; and the increase in the price per cask from 800-900 livres to 1,100-1,200 livres.

THE QUART LATOUR AFFAIR

Although the Revolution affected the other great wine-making estates such as Lafite and Margaux, it miraculously spared Latour. Its main owners had not emigrated, which saved the vineyard from being administered by managers imposed upon the estate, most of whom were incompetent. However, the Comte de Ségur-Cabanac had emigrated, and so his share was nationalised and sold at auction on 12 Messidor of year an IV according to the Revolutionary calendar (1796), for the sum of 219,724 livres, to Jeanne Courregeolles-Teulon and Dr. Monbalon.

During the Revolution, the estate lost money because it was extremely difficult to sell the wine. Business improved, however, under the Directory (1795-1799), when profits rose to 25 per cent. Nevertheless, the Ségur heirs did not fully understand the financial importance of the Latour estate. In 1790, they declined the offer made by the Comte de Ségur-Cabanac, who before emigrating had suggested selling them his share of Latour. Nor did they bid in the 1796 auction, though they may have been intimidated by the excesses of the Jacobin Revolution. Two years later, the new owners of the *quart Latour*, were trying to find a buyer, and even then there was no reaction from the other owners, and the negotiations which the broker undertook on behalf of the Comte de la Pallu never came to fruition. In the first half of the nineteenth century, the rest of the Latour property became divided up through inheritances, and opportunities for purchases presented themselves at regular intervals, yet each time the Ségur heirs failed to take advantage of the opportunity and seemed happy to share their inheritance with others.

Latour continued to thrive. The profit and loss account had been in the black since 1750, and probably even earlier, since the bad years had been very rare and the profits easily covered these rare losses. Between 1784 and 1823, the shareholders' income from profits totalled more than FF1,800,000, an average profit of about 15 per cent. Furthermore, this period saw a considerable increase, of between 200 and 300 per cent, in the capital value.

The new owners of Latour included the famous wine-merchants Pierre-François Guestier and Nathanaël Barton, who bought thirteen shares in 1833, and Nathaniel Johnston, another important merchant, who purchased the same number of shares in 1840. In the preceding year, the thirteen shares of the late Dr. Monbalon had been divided among the Ségur heirs, who finally took the opportunity of increasing their holdings, and the Guestier-Barton duo. The complex play of shares and inheritances eventually led to the property value being calculated in 144ths!

The number of wine merchants buying into the property was gradually growing. For instance, long before he was a shareholder, Nathaniel Johnston had contributed to the budget of the estate in order to pay the costs of cultivation. This aspect of the management of the estate is surprising; the fraudulent activities of the estate manager Lamothe, which had been discovered, and a probable lack of proper supervision by the owners still do not explain why the profitable years — that is to say, every year since the demise of Lamothe, with the exception of 1838 — did not cover the cost of cultivation.

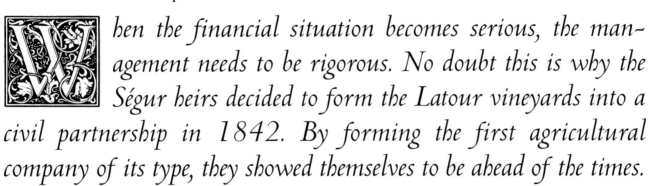 *hen the financial situation becomes serious, the management needs to be rigorous. No doubt this is why the Ségur heirs decided to form the Latour vineyards into a civil partnership in 1842. By forming the first agricultural company of its type, they showed themselves to be ahead of the times.*

The trading side of the estate deliberately fenced in the owners and "eroded" the Latour estate. This put the other owners in a dangerous position. The wine merchants, who had become shareholders, were paid their dividends in the form of wine — Latour wine, of course. For this reason, it was in their interest to ensure that wholesale prices were low, because they would make a bigger profit on reselling the wine than the amount they might have lost on their dividends.

The three Bordeaux wine merchants held 29/144ths of Latour. Furthermore, they had advanced money to the Ségur heirs to enable them to buy the Monbalon shares, and had pledged about FF150,000 for the costs of cultivation. When converted into shares, this represented no less than 52/144ths of the estate. This strategy began to bear fruit, which gave the Ségur heirs cause for concern.

In 1840, at the initiative of the Marquis de Courtivron, the heirs realised that they needed to abandon the arrangement whereby people outside the family had a share of the estate. Intricate calculations were required: if the estate was worth less than FF1,800,000, it ought not to be sold because it was bringing in more than FF80,000 net, based on sales of sixty casks per year at an average of FF1,750, not including the secondary wines. This

was clearly a very conservative estimate of the yield as it works out at 5 or 6 per cent less than the normal profitability. If the estate was worth more than FF 1,800,000, all the shares in it should be sold, since the profitability ratio would be insufficient.

Using this reasoning, the Ségur heirs decided to put the whole estate up for auction, and none were required to remain part-owners. The sale was held on 4 August 1841 in the auction rooms belonging to the Bordeaux notaries, and the bidding started at FF1, 200,000. Pierre-François Guestier was present. He had not considered buying because he believed, wrongly, that the Ségur heirs would try and push the bidding to the limit. He merely wanted to be sure that the wine merchants did not lose money as, having spent FF300,000 to acquire 29/144ths, they would not be happy unless the income from the sale exceeded FF1,500,000. The highest bidder proved to be the Comte Léon de Beaumont, who bid on behalf of the Ségur heirs, and the price was FF1,511,000.

It is surprising that the wine merchants adopted this "wait-and-see" policy since once it became clear that the Ségur heirs intended to buy out the entire Latour estate, it was in their interest to increase the bidding in order to make a bigger profit from their shares. The most likely explanation is that, despite their financial position, they were not able to take the risk of being the winning bidders.

At any event, the Ségur heirs finally succeeded in reversing the consequences of the Revolution (the sale of national treasures) and regained their independence by eliminating the participation of outsiders. However, the operation was extremely costly since buying out the wine merchants' shares, complicated by the reimbursement of advances and the liquidation of rights, miscellaneous interests, etc., represented a disbursement of FF612,056.95. The Courtivron, Beaumont and Flers families borrowed money at 5 per cent

Above: The Château Latour arms on display in the wall encircling the estate.

Opposite: A mature vine stock.

44

interest, while the only Ségur heir who did not appear to need to get into debt was the Marquis de Fayet. Once the property ownership problem had been cleared up, in 1842 the Ségur heirs created a civil partnership, called *la Société civile du vignoble de Latour*. Although these aristocrats were from a deeply traditionalist background, this was the first agricultural partnership of its type to be founded in France. The owners would subsequently supervise the running of the estate, limit expenditure and generally keep a closer eye on the operation. This shrewd financial move put an end to a time when the power exercised by estate managers was leading to an anarchic situation elsewhere in French agriculture. Between 1842 and 1853, the vineyard operated without cashflow. Funds were so scarce that overheads had to be covered by taking out short-term loans, and as late as 1854 there was a heavy mortgage on the property. This difficult situation explains the reappearance of Barton and Guestier, who offered the Ségur heirs a ten-year commitment. The wine merchants undertook to purchase the entire yield over the period at the set price of FF1,750 per cask.

*appy vineyards, like nations, have no history. The Ségur heirs ran the Latour estate efficiently and skilfully, especially since the income from it was no less than spectacular. Nothing seemed to affect their prosperity which continued serenely for thirty years.*

A contract of this nature indicates that the merchants had enormous confidence in the quality of the wines of future years. They imposed only two restrictions: manuring was to be limited to one-twentieth of the vineyard annually, and the annual replantings should not exceed one-fortieth of the vineyard. In other words, low yields from old vines. For their part, the owners were counting on regular, large-scale production of around seventy-five casks – an over-estimation, as the average production for the ten years of the contract was sixty-eight casks, slightly less than for the previous period. They were also banking on production costs remaining stable, which, in general, turned out to be the case.

The wine merchants found the arrangement very satisfactory and suggested renewing the contract after the ten years had expired. After discussing the matter at the partnership board meeting, the owners rejected the offer, and they were right to do so, even though they were losing security. In fact, this arrangement was only of interest to the owner if he was able to produce a large amount of wine, while the wine merchant was counting on market forces which would also take account of the quality of the wine and the rarity of certain vintages. The less wine there was, the higher the price, but the owners would suffer, only having a limited number of casks to sell and always at a set price.

The Ségur heirs managed to avoid this trap in the years after the contract had ended. As a result of the effects of oidium (fungus wilt) which attacked the crop in 1852, the volume of production for the years 1854 to 1857 was well below average (13, 35, 31 and 49 casks respectively), and the price per cask soared. Prices were FF5,000, FF2,800, FF5,000 and FF4,400 respectively, although the contract would have been for FF1,750. These very high prices were the saving of estates in the Médoc but did little to enrich the owners for two reasons, namely, the low yield (on average 32 casks), and the increased expenditure involved in fighting the disease. In 1859, rains and hail during flowering again reduced production (41 casks at FF2,750); in 1860 the harvest was abundant but of poor quality (109 casks at FF550).

In 1855, the great Bordeaux wines received their official classification though this had little effect on the wine trade at the time. For more than fifty years, the Bordeaux brokers had been using their own private or public classifications and the 1855 classification was merely official recognition of this fact.

After 1861, Latour went through an exceptional period. This was not a one-off as in the surprise year of 1858 (111 casks at FF4,800), but a long period of more than thirty years of good harvests, negotiated at unheard-of prices, as the table below shows:

Year	Casks	Price in FF	Year	Casks	Price in FF
1854	13	5,000	1868	99	6,250
1855	35	2,800	1869	125	3,200
1856	31	5,000	1870	128	3,000
1857	49	4,400	1871	123	1,800
1858	111	4,800	1872	113	1,200
1859	41	2,750	1873	94	2,250
1860	109	550	1874	190	5,500
1861	87	5,000	1875	165	4,000
1862	82	4,000	1876	62	2,400
1863	74	2,000	1877	154	2,600
1864	115	4,500	1878	133	4,000
1865	126	5,600	1879	67	2,500
1866	109	700	1880	63	3,800
1867	74	1,200			

For instance, despite two appalling harvests, due to cold wet weather (1860 and 1866), production averaged more than 100 casks and the average price of a cask was FF3,300. The Ségur heirs were thus extremely wise to reject the 1853 offer to renew the contract, which had been based on an annual forecast of 68 casks at FF1,750 per cask.

INVESTMENT AND EXPANSION

The management of a *grand cru* requires a certain amount of flexibility. One ought not to be forced to sell the result of a harvest on poor terms, with the excuse that there is nowhere to store it. Yet Latour had long been handicapped by lack of space, and the estate rented storage cellars in Bordeaux and elsewhere for keeping their unsold wine. There was an urgent need for a long-term store, which was built in 1860 to hold about four hundred casks, but from the outset proved to be slightly too small. Subsequently, and while wine was selling at a good price, Latour embarked on a series of building and renovation works. For example, a wall was built to enclose the estate, the wine stores were enlarged and premises were built for the harvest workers, which included a ballroom, since at Latour, a band was hired to play for harvest dances. The most important building work was planned in 1864. For several centuries, no trace of the fortress had remained at Latour. In 1842, the operating partnership took the name of *Société civile du vignoble de Latour* rather than *Château Latour* because nothing remained of the château. So little suitable accommodation remained on the estate that the owners could not live there. All that was available was one damp, dilapidated room (hence the excess of freedom allowed to the estate managers). The owners mostly remained in Bordeaux, and lack of suitable transport

Above: Animal pulling power at Latour.

also disinclined them to visit Latour. However, once the estate manager Lamotte had died, and the property was once again run by the owners, they stayed longer and more often at Latour. It was lack of funds alone which had delayed the building of a country house, a French château. The rank of *premier cru* awarded in 1855 required that a residence be built which matched the social status of the owners.

The tiny harvest of 1857 (49 casks) and the size and quality of the fine harvest of 1858 had brought in FF550,000. The planned château, which had been delayed hitherto, was now a possibility. A FF50,000 loan was obtained for this purpose, showing how profitable Latour had become. The revenue from these two harvests would have financed the construction of ten châteaux. Later harvests were even better; the 1874 harvest was an exceptional one, it is true, but it would have paid the cost of twelve châteaux, while the average annual net profit during this golden age would have made it possible to build and furnish three châteaux a year.

Duphot, a Bordeaux architect who had built other châteaux, which were springing up like mushrooms at the time, was set to work. He produced some ambitious plans which the owners considered to be too costly, not knowing that thirty fat years lay before them. The Marquis de Beaumont-Villemauzy commissioned a small building, half the size of the one suggested by Duphot. Instead of the sixteen rooms initially planned, they built eight. However, the finest quality materials which Duphot recommended were used for the construction. The quantity survey came to more than FF45,000, plus another three or four thousand francs for furnishings. The result was the building which stands on the estate today.

Happy vineyards, like nations, have no history. The Ségur heirs ran the Latour estate efficiently and skilfully, especially since the income from it was no less than spectacular. Nothing seemed to affect their prosperity, which continued serenely for thirty years. Such success is not mere chance. The volume produced needs to be constant, the quality of the wine needs to be maintained, the costs of production must be kept under control and the selling price per cask must not be allowed to fall. Apart from the effects of adverse weather conditions, the producers controlled quality and quantity. Had they not managed to overcome oidium in difficult circumstances? On the other hand, they could not control production costs and the caprices of the market, which dictate the price per cask, and were even less manageable. The only room they had to manoeuvre was by refusing to sell at a low price, but even this was a strategy which could only be used on occasion.

It would be naive to imagine that these factors were independent of each other. They are closely linked, so much so that their effects are generally cumulative and their consequences are amplified, thus making the market for wine ever more sensitive. For example, a drop in quality causes an immediate drop in price. On the other hand, if the quantity is reduced, the price of wine rises, falling again if there is an abundant harvest. Having

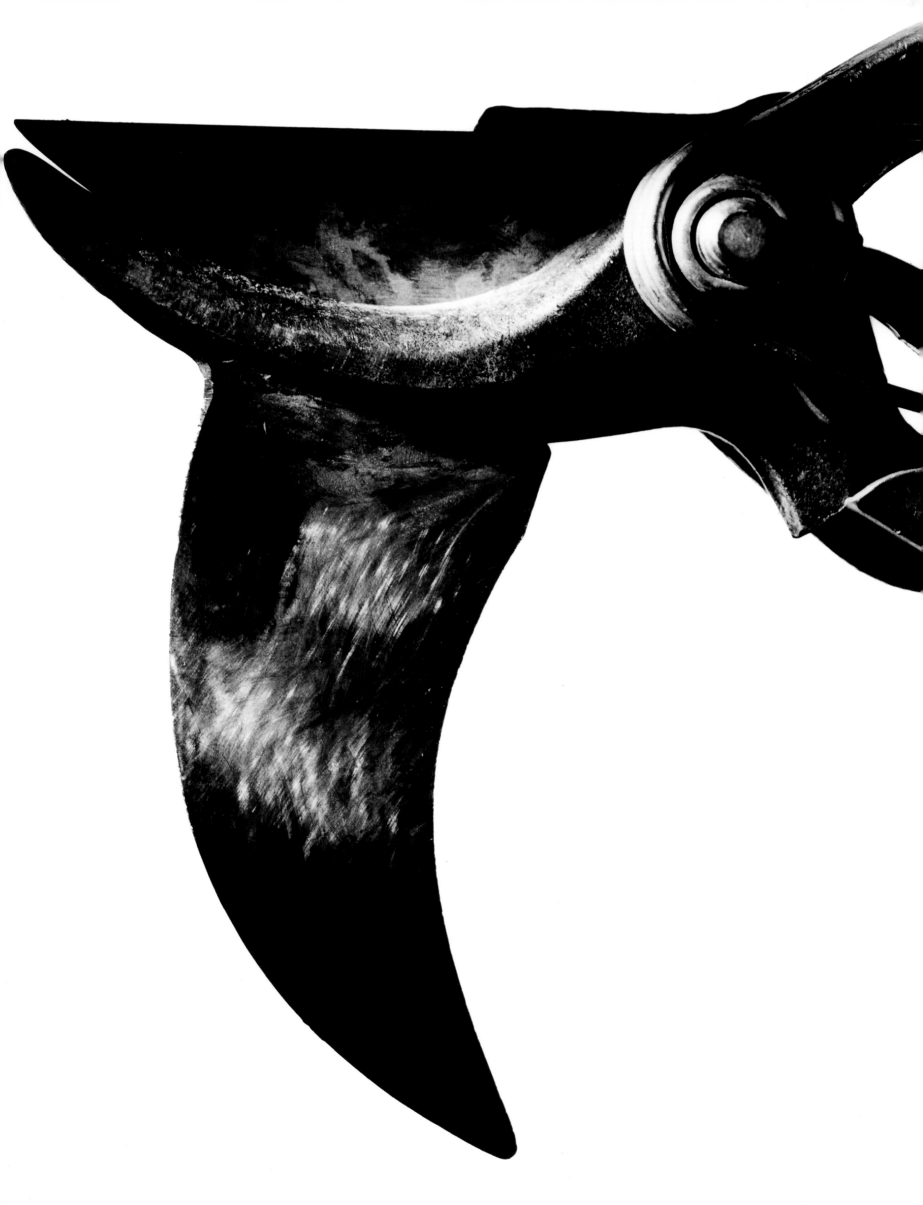

too much wine of mediocre quality, as happened in 1860 and 1866 is catastrophic. Disaster is avoided as soon as one factor comes into play against another, for instance, where the vintage is not outstanding but the amount produced is limited. This was the situation in 1855 and 1856.

The golden age began with the happy combination of a high price for wine (due to strong demand thanks to favourable economic conditions and the rarity value of the wines as a result of small harvests) and the quantities produced.

The decline began due to the reduction in the harvest. The fifteen years prior to 1879 had been good years for the grape harvest, producing more than 126 casks, but in the next eight years the harvest fell by half. Two calamities were responsible: phylloxera of the vine, which first appeared in 1880, and mildew, a fungus disease which was discovered at Latour in 1882.

Contrary to what is normally supposed, mildew did more damage to the vines than phylloxera. Bordeaux Mixture (copper sulphate) came into use in 1886, saving the vineyard and the yield per hectare, and production increased enormously after 1888. The owners might have thought their troubles were at an end — or better still that they had repeated their success after the oidium scare, because their battle against that fungus mould had caused production to climb from 58 to 100 casks. Production at the turn of the century increased from 826 hectolitres to 1,095 hectolitres on average. However, this did not do the owners much good for three reasons, namely, the increase in the cost of production, the decrease in the quality of the wine and the collapse in the price per cask.

The health of a company can be measured by the ratio between income and expenditure. The following table is, in this respect, very enlightening:

Income	Expenditure (production cost, as percentage of income)
1879-1887	61%
1888-1897	61%
1898-1907	87%
1908-1917	93.5%
1918-1921	105%

It is easy to see why the owners were considering selling the estate in late 1889; an option was even signed by the Vicomte de Courtivron. The Ségur heirs had shown signs of a desire to rid themselves of Latour during the first half of the nineteenth century, but no serious offer had ever been made to them. This was probably the first time that a notary was forwarding an offer in the region of FF3 million. The owners were stunned and most of them readily agreed — but the sale never happened as the purchaser did not follow through.

The civil partnership was organised in such a way that strangers could not have a say in the running, but shares were put up for sale. The memory of the purchase of the *quart*

Latour remained vivid, however, and the company reserved the right of pre-emption should a similar circumstance arise.

Between 1886 and 1898, the Ségur heirs put 23 shares up for sale. The partnership decided to buy them and this increased the value of the other shares, since the partnership's capital was no longer divided into 144, but into 121 shares; nevertheless, in order to be able to afford to purchase the 23 shares, the partnership had to subscribe to loans, just as it had taken out a loan in 1893 to ensure that the estate was properly run and to cover the rebuilding of the wine stores, which were damaged by fire in 1892.

The century ended in pessimistic mood. The management of Château Latour had always made it a priority to maintain the best production conditions, to protect the reputation and image of Latour. The board meetings of the *Société civile du vignoble de Latour* did not always go smoothly. There is always a conflict of interest between investments to be made and dividends to be paid. Different strategies are required according to whether the present or the future is the priority. Sometimes decisions are all the harder to make when the very survival of the vineyard depends upon being right about the way the market will move, since there is so much room for error.

In the late nineteenth century, the Comte Guillaume de Beaumont opted for an increase in production, but in 1892, the price per cask fell by half. He had wanted to keep turnover high and there had been little choice in the way to achieve this since all the other producers of *crus classés* (classified growths) were pursuing the same course of action. Although this was not necessarily the right choice under the circumstances, a producer could not adopt an individual strategy, since he was hostage to the price of wine on the market.

It was not until all the wine producers realised that the price had collapsed (prices had fallen by a third and even as much as a half), that they devoted themselves to reducing production. The price per cask rose but revenue was not greatly affected. It was then that a number of wine merchants offered contracts to the Médoc wine producers, who were tired of having to work so hard to make a sale and needed to reduce their stock.

The Latour experience of contracts had not been a particularly happy one, but the memory was fading (1843-1853) and Jouet, a go-ahead estate manager, encouraged the owners to accept, especially as the price of FF1,650 per cask offered was a great deal more than the average price over the previous fifteen years (FF1,265). Finally, the Comte de Beaumont signed a contract for five harvests, from 1906 to 1910, with a limitation on yield, namely that if the harvest yielded more than 120 casks, the additional casks would fetch only FF825 each (the other *premiers crus* of the Médoc district were contracted for the same price, but only for ten years).

 *he owners tried to persuade the wine merchants to change their contract prices, but the latter claimed that the contracts had been entered into in good faith and that there was no reason to change them. Since the courts would probably have upheld the wine merchants' case, the proposed price review failed.*

When the contract expired, the possibility of its renewal arose, though at a higher price, as prices were improving, though they still could not be considered "high". Jouet was instructed by the owners to ask for FF2,500 a cask, but this was not accepted and the contract was not renewed. Latour thus found itself once again free of commitments, which proved to be providential since most of the vintages sold for at least FF2,500 a cask until war broke out in 1914.

The reduction in staff due to mobilisation coincided with another attack of oidium wilt. This time, it could not be overcome, due to lack of manpower, since vines could only be treated manually. As a result, the 1915 harvest was completely declassified and in any case, the yield was very small (38 casks). Many of the Bordeaux vineyards were not even harvested, something which had never happened before.

The 1915 declassification was almost fortunate, as the firm of Echenauer had contracted to acquire the total vintages of 1914 and 1915 for FF2,200 a cask. In view of the

Following double-page: Celebrating the end of harvest.

mediocre quality of the harvest, the only way the Latour reputation could be defended satisfactorily was by eradicating the 1915 production. It was thus agreed to replace the 1915 harvest with the 1916, and the wine made in 1915 was quite simply never sold.

The Château Lafite and the Château Margaux contracts ended in 1917. The brokers wanted to continue the system and suggested a new contract to the three *premiers crus* vineyards at the same price of FF2,650. In the case of Château Latour, the Comte de Beaumont signed the contract in July 1917. The war continued, and while prices were just about acceptable, the cost of benefits, wages and land prices continued to rise.

This time, the vagaries of production and the market greatly favoured the wine merchants. The year 1917 was a good vintage and prices rose steeply, with Latour wine selling for more than FF4,000 the cask. The brokers, who were making a profit of FF1,350 on each cask, were even happier with the great vintage of 1918, which they resold for about FF6,000. But the wine of 1919 smashed every record, with some casks fetching as much as FF8,000. And yet despite the boom, the estate owners were still only earning FF2,650 under the terms of their contracts.

This situation could not last, since the profits made by the wine merchants were not helping the producers. The latter continued to have to deal with a variety of problems but all they had was a limited steady income. The problems included an increase in the price of sulphur, copper sulphate and oak wood as well as serious social unrest (an agricultural workers' strike lasted for several months in early 1920). Everything seemed to be aimed at ruining the estates, whose wines were selling at such high prices. The owners tried to persuade the wine merchants to change their contract prices, but the latter claimed that the contracts had been entered into in good faith and that there was no reason to change them.

Since the courts would probably have upheld the wine merchants' case, the proposed price review failed. As a result, in order to be able to escape from the local trading conditions in Bordeaux, Latour entered into direct selling contracts (with Nicolas in 1923) and even into contracts with wine merchants outside Bordeaux (in 1924 and 1925). In the same spirit, in 1924 Philippe de Rothschild suggested that in future, wine should only be sold in bottles, to prevent any fraud. However, this was also a way of changing the way things had been done in the past.

The very great vintages of 1928 and 1929 were easily sold by Latour at a very high price (FF20,000 a cask). As the 1930s dawned, the Latour estate was in funds, and was even doing well, since the reserve funds were increasing. If the payment by instalments of the 1928 and 1929 sales are taken into account, Latour had about FF3,300,000 at its disposal. This was more than fortunate because the Wall Street Crash of 1929 was to cause a huge upheaval in the European economy, and destroy the 1931 market.

If the wine-merchants were to be believed, during the depression that followed the Crash, it was not a question of price but of the fact that the demand was no longer there. To make matters worse, the harvests were terrible between 1930 and 1933. Even the abolition of Prohibition in the United States in 1933 did not revive the moribund market because the dollar had lost a lot of its value. The decline continued. The board of directors took draconian measures, as they had in the years 1884-1886 and between 1900 and 1904, and no dividend was paid in 1932, 1933, 1934 or 1935 (they were to pass the same resolution in 1946, 1947 and 1948).

In 1934, a good harvest revived the market slightly but political and social events, followed by the advent of the left-wing *Front populaire* government, did little to improve business.

Above and opposite: Pruning.

The market was very flat right up until World War II, the only high point being the sale of the 1934 vintage. Yet shrewd financial management enabled Latour to pay off its last loan, which had been taken out almost forty years previously.

If 1935 and 1936 were not brilliant years, 1937 saw the prices seesaw between FF12,000 and FF15,000. To dispose of harvests of poor quality, Latour again avoided using the services of Bordeaux wine merchants and introduced a new form of contract with a certain La Chevalerie. The sale price was fixed annually and took the costs of production into account. Furthermore, Latour reserved the right to sell to Bordeaux wine merchants at the same time, if the latter could offer a price which was at least 20 per cent higher than the price agreed with La Chevalerie. This system compensated Latour handsomely for the disastrous contract into which it had entered in the years 1917-1919. Sales were excellent: FF12,800 and FF15,000 for the 1935 and 1936 vintages, which in terms of quality were barely satisfactory.

In the spring of 1937, while the Comte de Beaumont was negotiating this contract outside Bordeaux in the greatest secrecy – the slightest indiscretion would have scuppered the whole deal – an extraordinary general meeting of shareholders was held. After four years without dividends, morale was at an all-time low, especially as poor sales were expected for the 1935 and 1936 harvests. In 1933 shares in the company were valued at FF8,000, compared with FF28,000 in 1928. In other words, in the space of just a few years, the shareholders had lost two-thirds of their capital.

The crisis was not restricted to Château Latour; all the wine producers were in serious difficulty. "The whole of Médoc is up for sale", wrote the press at the time. Other famous *crus*, such as Haut-Brion and Cheval Blanc at Saint-Émilion, were already on the market and yet there were hardly any buyers. The only option seemed to be to sell the wine at a wretchedly low price, which would cause even more losses. But the Comte de Beaumont finally persuaded the shareholders not to sell, and they ended by voting to continue the existence of the non-trading company for another ninety-nine years until 2036.

The outbreak of hostilities in 1939 ended the contract between Latour and La Chevalerie. The war had contradictory effects. After the Courtivrons, Hubert de Beaumont became chairman of the board and lived in the château. Manpower became scarce, as did food, and chemicals were hard to obtain. The German invasion in July 1940 was marked by the pillage of the Latour cellar and the theft of almost FF45,000 worth of wine. Subsequently, the German authorities purchased their wine, buying about thirteen million bottles of all types of Bordeaux wine, but in addition to this, wine was confiscated from sequestrated estates belonging to Jewish or British owners.

"*The whole of Médoc is up for sale", wrote the press at the time. The sellers were legion, the buyers non-existent or almost so. The Comte de Beaumont had to explain all this to the shareholders since many of them wanted to sell Latour ... but who would buy it?*

To tell the truth, the wine trade was not affected by the war. In fact, it was even revitalised. In 1940, the Latour wines sold at FF30,000 a cask; the Vichy government then forcibly fixed the price of wine, giving rise to a black market which caused the value of each cask to increase to up to FF130,000.

The great post-war vintages (1945-1947) did little to benefit the estate since the price of wine had been controlled in preceding years (1943-1944) at FF100,000 a cask; in addition, exports were taxed, the costs of production increased considerably, and the market was very flat. It is thus hardly surprising that Latour's balance sheets showed a deficit and no dividend was paid between 1946 and 1948.

Based on a stock valued at FF21 million, the company took out a loan in 1948 for FF5 million from the Crédit Foncier bank. Once again, a long period of prosperity dawned for the Bordeaux region in general and for Latour in particular. The great 1949 vintage caused the tensions to relax. Latour was able to sell half its stock and the owners

Following pages: Pruning the vines and harvesting scene.

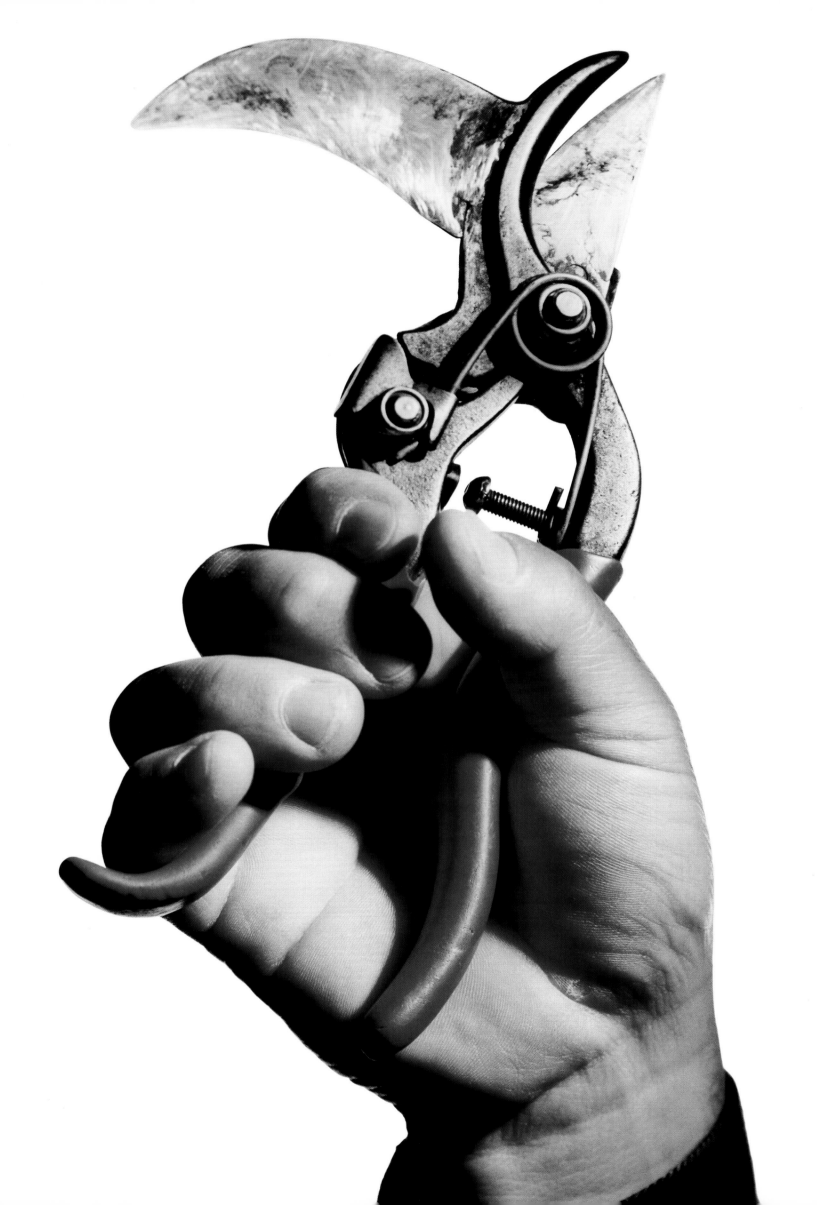

could once again draw a dividend (FF1,000 per share). In 1950, in certain sales, prices rose up to FF400,000 and even FF500,000 per cask.

The economic climate was favourable and, despite a slight setback in 1952, the good vintages – 1952, 1953, with 1955 even better (a selling price of FF700,000 per cask) – buoyed up by a new export boom, heralded a new golden age. The dividend was increased to FF142,000 per share. This is a surprisingly high figure, but the cumulative effect already mentioned should be taken into account. The price per cask had multiplied sevenfold in just a few years, while production had doubled in quantity (80 casks in 1947, 170 casks in 1955). From now on, nothing could deter the buyers, who seemed to be bewitched. Even the average-to-poor 1960 vintage was sold at 10,000 new francs, equivalent to one million old francs. The 1961 vintage was legendary, and assisted by a very small harvest of 63 casks, achieved the record price of 20,000 new francs a cask.

 *his sale, at a time of great prosperity, and after nearly three centuries of ownership, of huge profits, as well short periods when no dividends were distributed, caused enormous surprise. Yet the majority decision of the Ségur heirs was understandable.*

The Comte Hubert de Beaumont, who had spent the war at Latour and who had been forced to inform the shareholders that no dividend would be declared for the years 1946, 1947 and 1948, had the pleasure at the end of 1962 of offering a dividend of 3,000 new francs per share; it was the highest dividend ever paid.

In that same year of 1962, a group of British buyers made an offer to Latour. After lengthy negotiations, the extraordinary general meeting held on 22 January 1963 agreed to the sale and the transfer of the majority shareholding to the new partners. The last time the estate had been sold was in 1670 (the auction sale of 1841 was not an actual change of ownership). This sale – at a time of great prosperity, and after nearly three centuries of ownership, of huge profits, as well short periods when no dividends were distributed – came as an enormous surprise, even though there had been short periods when no dividends had been declared. Yet the majority decision of the Ségur heirs was understandable. They knew that it was impossible to sell wine during a slump unless they sold off their shares and that slumps occurred on a regular basis. Though some years offered exceptional capital gains (FF2,500 to FF75,000 in 1962), long periods of prosperity were rare and frequently the benefits were fleeting. Finally, the distribution of shares as a result of legacies had resulted in complicated, and even inextricable, situations, and certain heirs were strongly in favour of selling their shares under the right conditions.

Opposite: Wine merchant's label (1878).

Share capital of the non-trading company, the number of whose shares had increased through bequests, was divided as follows:

de Beaumont branch	77 shares	24 holders
de Courtivron branch	69 shares	30 holders
de Flers branch	9 shares	14 holders
Total	155 shares	68 holders

It should be explained that while sixty-two people held eighty-nine shares, six people – four Beaumonts and two Courtivrons – accounted for sixty-six, making up 42.5 per cent of the share capital. The fact that the holdings were so unequal also caused frequent conflicts of interest

Although the vineyard was very well tended, nevertheless, in technical terms, Latour was closer to the nineteenth than to the twentieth century, and the estate manager was getting on in years. Production needed to be modernised, some expensive new methods needed to be introduced and most of the shareholders were not inclined to spend the money. At all events, on 22 January 1963, 75 per cent of the shares were acquired by two British limited companies. Fifty per cent went to the Pearson Group, owned by Lord Cowdray, via its subsidiary, Hallminster Ltd., and 25 per cent to Harveys. The Comtes Hubert and Philippe de Beaumont represented the 25 per cent of shares which the Ségur heirs still owned on the board of directors. Under the chairmanship of David Pollock, major works were undertaken which cost nearly FF4.5 million, and of which two-thirds were self-financed. If the majority of Ségur heirs believed that the 1950s were merely a fleeting moment of prosperity, they were mistaken. The estate continues to flourish to the present day, if one excludes the brief downturn of 1973-1974. Once again the long-term has favoured the owners of Latour. Not only has production reached record levels – even the smallest harvests exceeding the largest volumes previously achieved – but the best price per cask achieved by the former ownership was exceeded by the lowest price recorded by the new owners (FF25,000 during the economic downturn of 1973-1974), with the exception of the miserable harvest of 1968 (FF18,000 all the same, and nearly 300 casks). Without going into detail, production doubled and the price per cask increased at least fifteenfold, several times twentyfold. The record dividend declared in 1962 by the Comte de Beaumont looks quite small at FF3,000 per share when compared to the figures achieved in the years 1980-1988, of more than FF120,000 per share. In terms of the stable franc values of the period, these figures translate into an increase of more than 660 per cent.

By abandoning the family firm in order to step into the world of international capitalism, Latour had become more dynamic but had take the risk of turning into just another commercial venture. Thus, in 1990, after twenty-seven years of stability, Latour partially changed hands once again.

Allied-Lyons, which already owned 25 per cent of the shares (via Harveys), took control and spent £58 million on the estate, increasing its overall value to £110 million. This increase in capital caused a proportional increase in the price per share, which had been fixed at FF2,500 in 1961, attaining FF75,000 F in 1963 (the initial offer had been for FF65,000). Each share was now worth FF7,067,420! The Pearson Group, quite apart from the dividends it had received, had multiplied its capital twelvefold. The Allied-Lyons takeover also broke the final bond between the Ségur heirs and Latour, since the Comte Philippe de Beaumont sold his remaining share in this transaction. He died three years later.

Allied-Lyons profited from two excellent vintages (1989 and 1990) but a downturn in international trade dampened their enthusiasm. In 1990, the dividend per share amounted to nearly FF250,000. In 1991, it was almost FF300,000. The years 1991 to 1993, however, brought in average profits, disappointing yields, and unspectacular vintages. In 1993, Allied-Lyons finally sold Latour to Artémis S.A., that is to say to François Pinault, for the sum of FF735 million. But the wine-makers themselves remain a permanent fixture. The continuity of Château Latour is in the hands of the practitioners, not the owners, who are more in the service of the estate than vice versa. It would be easy to show that the *premier cru* is in charge, and the owner merely bends to its will.

In any case, there is little room for manoeuvre by the owner or the technicians, in view of the imperatives of production, the health of the vine, the universal introduction of new techniques and the demands of the marketplace.

Since modernisation during the Pearson management, Latour has had no serious financial worries, at least if the price which the wines fetch is anything to go by. The Allied-Lyons takeover had little effect on the way in which the estate was run. Since François Pinault acquired Latour, it can be said that he obeys the rule defined by a famous politician: change within continuity. Of course, in 1994 he sold Ulysse Cazabonne, a small wine merchant's established in 1976 by Jean-Paul Gardère with Henri Martin and Jean Cordier, which Gardère ran between 1977 and 1984, until it was bought by Latour (1984-1990). He also built a tractor shed (1997) and a wine store which could hold eight hundred thousand bottles (1998), but none of this affects the quality of the wine. To paraphrase a famous saying, it can happily be said: "Latour I was, Latour I am, Latour I shall remain."

THE
GREAT ESTATE
MANAGERS
OR THE RECOGNITION OF SKILL

e have described the succession of owners who preserved the integrity of Latour over the centuries and who controlled the destiny of the estate. Yet their vigilance could never have been rewarded without the daily activity of foreword-thinking estate managers who were directly responsible for managing the vineyard and making the wine. This chapter runs parallel to the previous one, and shows how much today's Château Latour owes to them. In the late Middle Ages, the "Mayne de la Tor" already covered most of the current estate. This situation is rare enough to be worthy of special mention since it is the reason for one of the main characteristics of Latour — its continuity. The meadows ran along the banks of the Gironde as they do today. However, as far as we know, the vineyard only covered one-fifth of the actual property. The date, and even the period, of the first vine plantation at the Tour Saint-Maubert or the "Mayne de la Tor" are unknown, but there are indications that other crops and woods covered the rest of the land.

The complex status of the *co-seigneurie* of the estate makes it difficult to ascertain the destination of the wine produced in the Middle Ages. It satisfied the needs of the growers and paid their dues to the lords, who were given about one-fifth of the production. Contracts drawn up in the late fourteenth century stipulate that the wine must be "good, pure, clear", delivered in new casks, and that it must come only from the Saint-Maubert land holdings. This last condition was imposed upon the lord Amadieu de la Motte by Jean Treulo, who was in the habit of sending wines to England. It is an important one, since it could be interpreted as a recognition of the quality of wines from Saint-Maubert, the future Château Latour.

We have explained how the *co-seigneurie* became a single *seigneurie* on the initiative of the de Mullet family, and how the estate was consolidated by Denis de Mullet, making it possible to change from the multiple crops which tenant-farmers were required to grow, to the

Opposite: The dovecote, seen from inside the winery.

monoculture of the vine, which increased the value of the land holdings once the leases had been bought out. The running of a wine-producing estate is not the business of the landed gentry, especially not of a delegate to the parliament such as Denis de Mullet. He therefore hired an estate manager in the person of Pierre de Lalande, in late 1648. This new employee, who lived in a house owned by de Mullet at Saint-Laurent, was to be responsible for the estate and the sale of its produce.

Thus the first Latour estate manager enters history. He was to be followed by Breton-neau and Pebaret, then by Raymond de Saint-Ange, who was hired as an agent by Pierre Daulède de Lestonnac, and who ran the Seigneurie de Saint-Maubert acquired by Daulède de Lestonnac through marriage to Catherine de Mullet.

The grape-growing estates suffered a variety of fates in the seventeenth century. Although he also owned Margaux, Jean-Denis Daulède sold Latour in 1670, which in the long run brought the estate into Ségur ownership. The Lafite, Mouton and Calon estates suffered the same fate. Lafite and Latour were jointly administered and their wines sold at the same price by their shared "director", who was none other than the Pauillac notary, Souisse.

SOUISSE: THE AGING NOTARY

This concentration of great estates explains why the wines were listed by brokers in their purchase ledgers as Souisse-Lafite and Souisse-Latour. When the inheritance left by Nicolas-Alexandre de Ségur in 1763 was settled, the estates were separated. Lafite was bequeathed to his grandson, Nicolas-Marie-Alexandre de Ségur, while three of the daughters of the chief justice inherited Latour, despite the fact that they lived elsewhere.

Opposite: Cabernet grapes.
Following pages: Saw-edged knife used for tending vines.

Meanwhile, Souisse the notary continued to act as "director". The Lafite estate was managed by Domenger, while between 1755 and 1774, the Latour estate seems to have been left to its agricultural labourers, and no great plans were made for it. Eventually, the new owners hired a Parisian administrator, Lenain, and left Domenger to run both Lafite and Latour between 1774 and 1785.

DOMENGER: FROM LAFITE TO LATOUR

The estate manager is the life and soul of the property. He is responsible for running it efficiently, for the morale of those who work there, the competence of the skilled workers, the general health of the vineyard and the perfection of the wine.

During the last quarter of the eighteenth century, the organisation of the estate, which was run by Lenain from Paris, become more complex. A "man of business" administered the property locally, although it was Domenger who was responsible for running it, for the quality of the wine and for its sale. This division of roles can easily cause serious problems if the various administrators are not on the best of terms, and this is precisely what happened when Lenain sent Latour someone named Starpart whose abilities appear to have been limited. Starpart was not a success and was dismissed in 1777.

*he estate manager is the life and soul of a property. He is responsible for running it efficiently, for the morale of the employees and the competence of the skilled workers. The health of the vineyard and the perfection of the wine depend on him.*

It was then Domenger's turn to appoint a "man of business". He chose a local man, Lavie, but soon discovered that he was "the lowest scoundrel, constantly drunk", to quote one of his letters. Lavie only lasted a year and Lenain chose another "man of business", Pey Duc, who was not a good wine-maker. Domenger found that the 1784 vintage, which had excellent potential, was hard to sell, which infuriated Duc. Domenger now only visited Latour to taste the wines and refrained from intervening in any other way. This is why he failed to realise that Lenain and Duc had conspired together to divert Latour wines for their benefit and were engaged in other malpractices. When Duc died in 1785, his nephew, Mondon, succeeded him on the initiative of Domenger, who knew him as he had employed him at Lafite. Strangely, Mondon denounced his uncle's previous dishonesty although he himself had done the same thing at Lafite. Domenger was forced to remove him discreetly in order not to damage the reputation of the Latour wines.

After all these disappointments, Domenger finally found the right candidate, Bergé.

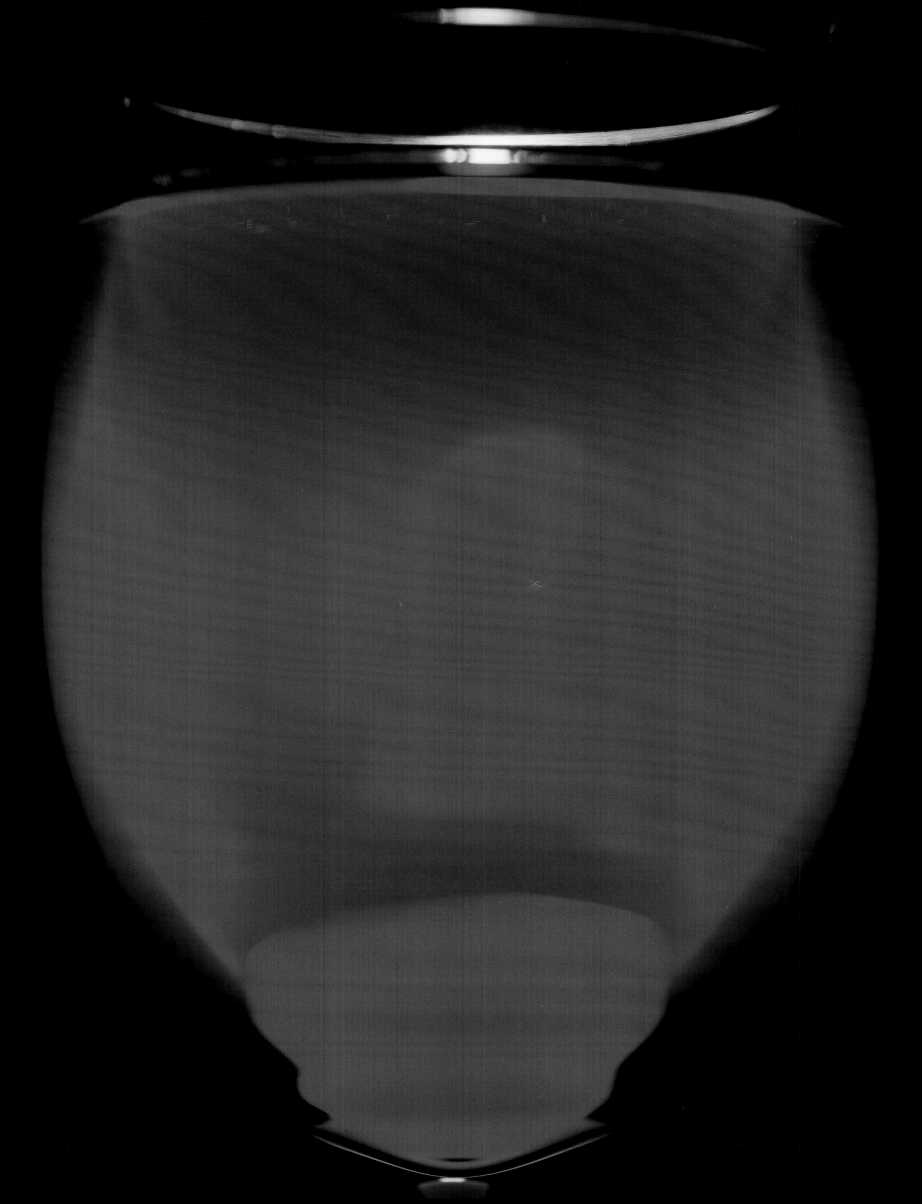

The political climate, however, made trading difficult. For example, Domenger had to try to avoid being paid in *assignats*, a promissory note which many creditors refused to accept. However, the minor vintages sold reasonably well between 1789 and 1794, and Domenger upheld the prestige of Latour until his death in 1797.

POITEVIN: THE CLEAR-SIGHTED ESTATE MANAGER

Poitevin succeeded Domenger as estate manager. He probably knew him personally, as both of them had family ties at Saint-Estèphe. Poitevin was of the same calibre as Domenger: he restored the vineyard and was an expert in vinification and wine-tasting. He was also on excellent terms with the Bordeaux wine merchants. Poitevin was realistic and shrewd, and he kept the key of the wine store in his pocket. The only person he trusted with it, if he went away, was his assistant Moreau.

Through the activities and work of Domenger and Poitevin, a good deal is known about the art of vine-growing and wine-making in the late eighteenth century. The amount of knowledge which the grape-growers had already acquired is surprising. In 1750 – and probably even earlier – the relationship between the soil type, vine stocks, climate and wine had been established. Whether or not as a result of this knowledge, the estate managers gained in importance in this era. They mastered the rudiments of geology, even if they only had an empirical understanding of it. The importance of gravel was realised, especially the gravel of Latour, which is mentioned on several occasions as being of just the right size. The benefits and disadvantages of water are also stated.

The ditches and drainage channels were regularly cleaned at Latour. A note was even made of those sites where the vines were not doing well. These were always places where "water had collected between two pieces of land", as Domenger wrote in 1789. These places were known as *mouillères*, patches where the clay was too compacted to allow water to drain away. The problem of unsuitable soil is interesting in that it makes it possible to measure the effect of market forces on the quality of production and vice versa. It was not until 1817 that it became technically possible to drain these waterlogged patches by using drainage pipes. This was a costly operation and involved investment, which presupposes that there was hope of earning a profit.

It was the hard work of the estate managers which created the gap between the future *premiers crus* and the lesser wines. They were not only more highly skilled but also capable of persuading the owners to invest in the property. They knew the price of wine and helped to fix it. They understood the pressure applied by the market to produce quality wines and thus worked hard to introduce improvements into the estate. They also initiated the system of secondary wines, which they distinguished from the *grand vin*, or "great wine". After 1750, the way in which the land was divided into plots at Latour inspired the

idea of a second crop. From then onwards, the best plantings were identified. Only sixteen plots produced the best wine, and the very best of them was known to be the *Grand Fort* on the Latour plateau, which had the best exposure and where the gravel was coarser, thus providing the most efficient drainage. These observations were used to determine the criteria which distinguished the great wine from the secondary wines; the latter were produced on those plots of land which were less favoured by nature. Of course, it might also be the case that a cask of great wine was not up to standard and might be downgraded to become a secondary wine. At least during that era, however, the opposite never occurred.

Almost as soon as Poitevin arrived, in early 1798, he planted another twenty thousand badly needed vine stocks. He knew that for the great wine, white grapes should be used only sparingly; some were kept, however, and a few barrels of white wine were even made for the owners' use. During the replantings, Poitevin noticed that one stock in three was missing and the white root-stocks were uprooted. Unfortunately, we do not know what varieties were planted or how densely. We know that Merlot was not used, because it did not make its appearance in Médoc until the nineteenth century. On the other hand, Cabernet and Malbec are mentioned by Poitevin, who was aware of the superiority of Cabernet and used it for the best plots. The vines were pruned and we are aware of what was done to improve the soil, methods perhaps even more successful than in the twentieth century when too many wines have fallen victim to soil enrichment.

From 1787, Mondon began to replace some poor Latour soil with good soil which he dug from ditches. Poitevin must have continued this operation because he sent a bill for several handcarts. On the other hand, whether for the sake of economy or caution, he did not use fertiliser. The Latour soil was not fertilised until after Poitevin's death in 1807, when his friend and successor Lamothe began regular spreading of organic manure, a practice which, up until then, had been restricted by Domenger to emergency treatment, such as in the aftermath of the terrible winter of 1789. Lamothe, on the other hand, favoured light fertilisation and stated in 1823 that manure must be used sparingly since it altered the quality of the soil and consequently that of the fruit.

Lamothe was by no means a typical estate manager, he had been a ship's captain before taking command of Latour. He was a great estate manager and a personality, although he had taken some liberties with pure and honest management of which the courts might not have taken a lenient view. Lamothe was Latour's first modern estate manager, and the enrichment of the soil is typical of his marked preference for a "businesslike approach", which was very much of the period in which he lived. He certainly cared about maintaining the quality of a great wine but he also wanted to improve production.

*t was not until Poitevin's successor's time that organic manure was used at Latour. But it was applied sparingly. After all, Lamothe had written in 1823 that manure must be used with caution since it altered the quality of the soil and consequently that of the fruit.*

Under Lamothe, the sites which had not been considered good enough for the production of great wine, were now used as soon as the grapes were ripe enough. He replanted vines, aimed to eliminate white grape stock, tried to save time, and eventually introduced grafting. He planted so much new stock that he ran short of seedlings and decided therefore to enlarge the Latour nursery, so that all seedlings could be grown on site. Naturally, the seedlings were thinned out and only the best young vines were chosen when it was pruning time. Another cultivation method was layering the vines and this was widely practised, especially on young stock.

Techniques improved for draining the soil, the importance of which has been mentioned earlier. The aim was always the same, namely to produce better wine and more of it. The early drainage pipes, installed in 1817 were made of pine. The last of the drains laid by Lamothe, who died in 1837, were hewn from stone and thus more resistant.

Opposite: A bottle of 1906 Grand Vin in the Château cellar.
Following pages: The cellar and an old poster announcing the sale at auction of eight hundred bottles of Château Latour.

ETUDES DE

Mᵉ Jacques VIALARD, licencié en droit, Notaire à Pauillac-Gironde
et Mᵉ MARTINI, Notaire à Fondettes (Indre-et-Loire)

VENTE

AUX ENCHERES PUBLIQUES

Le Samedi 22 Septembre à 10 heures du matin

à PAUILLAC, au Château Latour

DE 800 BOUTEILLES
de Château - Latour

1ᵉʳ Grand Crû du Médoc — ANNÉES DIVERSES

Dépendant de la Succession Bénéficiaire
de Madame la COMTESSE Charles de BEAUMONT

PAIEMENT COMPTANT : 23 % DE FRAIS EN SUS

Pour tous renseignements, s'adresser à

Mᵉ VIALARD, Notaire à Pauillac, Téleph. 15

Lesparre, Imprimerie M. MICHEL

The estate manager needed to maintain a balance between the investments needed to ensure quality and the constant need for profitability as the owners, who rarely visited the estate, were still entitled to reap its rewards. The income varied considerably, depending on the quality of the harvest and the price of wine, as was explained in the previous chapter.

THE ESTATE MANAGER AND VINIFICATION

The various financial, economic, climatic and commercial constraints restricted the activities of the estate manager and gave him little room to manœuvre, especially as he rarely dared to move off the beaten track. It was only when exceptional circumstances arose, such as a disastrous harvest, that he might decide to try a novel method. In normal times, the estate manager, sole master of the estate below God, would use the tried and tested vinification methods.

It would appear that between 1750 and 1950 vinification of the *grands crus* changed very little; the methods were more or less completely mastered – though of course only empirically – by 1750, a remarkable achievement. On the other hand, for reasons of style rather than through ignorance, scraping the grapes was only performed in bad years, when the wine took twice or three times the time recommended today to ferment in the vats.

It is the estate manager who decides on which day harvesting will begin, basing his judgement on the ripeness of the grapes which he tests by taste. Clearly, if the harvest is too soon, the wines will be uninteresting and green, but harvesting too late can also affect the quality. In 1798, which was a vintage year, Poitevin nevertheless notes: "The Lafite wine this year was lacking due to having been harvested too late". In 1802, having learned his lesson, he confirmed that "one must make haste as soon as the grape is ripe for fear of letting it overripen".

As is the case today, when rain threatened, the pace of work needed to be speeded up. In 1812, Lamothe completed the harvesting (of about 45 hectares or 135 acres) in five days, using 247 cutters and carriers. That year he was fortunate and the grapes ripened uniformly, but it was not uncommon to have to sort the grapes – and this was the greatest test for the estate manager, since he had no *tapis de tri,* the sorting cloth which had been greatly vaunted in recent years. Two centuries ago at Latour the estate manager would supervise the arrival of the grapes before pressing, making sure that any which were unripe or mouldy were removed. Traditionally, the grapes were not scraped, although it was suspected that unscraped grapes made the wine too acid. In 1808, Lamothe writes that Mr. Lynch "only loaded the vats with grapes which had been separated from their stalks". In 1812 and 1813, Lamothe used this method, but later returned to the old ways.

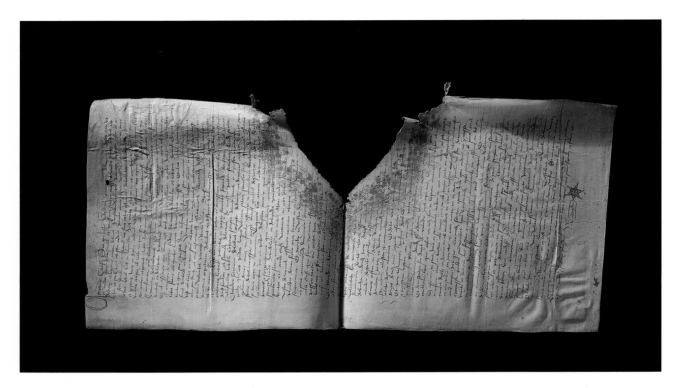

The fermentation time in the vat is worth investigating. At the time, again for reasons of tradition, finesse was considered more important than strength in a wine. Vat fermentation was thus short, and the wine was drawn off after about a week. In 1811, Lamothe fermented the wine in the vat for only five days, which could be interpreted as a dangerous flight of fancy. He clearly had his doubts as well but justified his action, explaining "[this] avoids more bitterness, which the wine inevitably acquires by fermenting longer in the vat with all the seeds and stalks". The wine must have been acceptable because it sold at the same price as all the other future *premiers crus*. In fact, short vat fermentation is still practised occasionally. In 1926, the Haut-Brion was vat-fermented for six days and it is still excellent.

The estate managers seem never to have been faced with the various misfortunes which can befall vinification, such as fermentation which runs riot, or other problems due to hot weather. There were, however, a few unlucky cold snaps, such as in 1817, which slowed fermentation. It is true that the potential alcoholic content was lower than it is today and that the vats had a smaller capacity, probably 45 to 50 hectolitres (twenty vats were needed to produce the average yield of less than 900 hectolitres).

Chaptalisation (adding sugar to increase the alcoholic content) had never been performed at Latour, but in 1816 Lamothe made an attempt to improve a rather poor vintage. He boiled up some must (unfermented wine) and dissolved 300 pounds of sugar in it, then poured the mixture into three vats (5 pounds per hogshead). However, he was dissatisfied with the result because he actually had too little sugar, which meant the alcoholic content only increased by half a degree whereas he had wanted to achieve 2.5°. He concluded resignedly "when Nature rejects the raw materials which make good quality wine, art can

Above and opposite: Old records from the estate.

Brouillard

Pour Mon Compte Courant

de l'an 1810
Du 1er Juillet

try its best to remedy the situation but will never achieve better than mediocrity".

Despite his careful tending of the great wines, Lamothe was much more careless, even daring, when it came to the secondary wines. For instance, he raised the alcoholic content of the secondary wine to "three-fifths" by adding alcohol. Many of his colleagues probably did the same, but he was breaking the law by modern standards.

Knowledge of the best maturing practices in the late eighteenth century was also surprisingly extensive. In the late fifteenth century, the "Dutch match" was introduced, a sulphur mixture which improved the keeping qualities of the wine. But sulphur has certain drawbacks. For it to work it needs to be used frequently, and if Dutch matches are burned too often, the wine becomes undrinkable. At the time, the wine was stored in hogsheads for dispatching, selling and consumption, but it was only supposed to remain in the hogshead for a few months. For this reason, the younger the wine, the dearer it was; if allowed to age in the hogsheads, the wine turned to vinegar. It was very difficult to find a drinkable wine in spring and even harder in summer.

In the sixteenth century, much research was done into preservation methods. Since the local brandies were so good, why not use them? Thus vinified wines were invented. These wines had a high alcoholic content (18°-22°) which suited wines which were naturally rich, but very different from what was required for Bordeaux wines.

In the late sixteenth and early seventeenth centuries, the solution was finally thought to have been found in ullage, whereby the hogshead was topped up once a week to compensate for evaporation. This also improved the wine. Indeed, ageing or *élevage* goes hand in hand with *tirage au fin*, whereby the lees are drawn off from the bottom of the cask, an innovation made by the creators of "vin Pontac" (Haut-Brion). They realised that when the lees had been drawn off, the wine needed topping up to replace the lost liquid. The same applied to drawing off wine to aerate and clarify it.

Domenger and his successors at Latour knew all these techniques and often replaced the *consume* (evaporated wine). The record books in the winery show how much wine had "flown away" and had to be replaced: the quantity was considerable and difficult to control. In 1778, the declared amount of topping up required amounted to twenty-five hogsheads. Domenger was astonished at this figure and suspected Pey Duc of theft, which was of course relatively easy when a natural loss must be compensated and it is impossible to determine precisely the volume concerned. Poitevin, who had no illusions as to the virtue of his contemporaries, wrote: "Whenever any topping up is to be done, it must be performed in my presence."

 *here there is topping up to compensate for a loss which cannot be measured precisely, all sorts of opportunities present themselves for diverting wine "for personal use". Poitevin had no illusions about his contemporaries and wrote: "Whenever any topping up is to be done, it must be performed in my presence."*

At Latour, wine for the owners' use was aged along with any wine that had been left over as unsold, which could happen due to poor vintages or as a result of war, trade embargoes, and so on. The miserable 1821 vintage did not find a buyer until 1834, and so remained in the wood for thirteen years. It was probably stored with the bung at the side, rather than at the top. This storage method had been adopted in the early eighteenth century as it was alleged to reduce evaporation and thus the need for topping up. In any case, Poitevin wrote that the Latour winery was too well ventilated, encouraging evaporation: he wanted to get the Chartrons merchants to take the wine and age it themselves because their wineries were better suited to the process. He also hoped they would do so before the first topping up after removal of the lees, since this would save 5 per cent of his wine.

Wine was always kept in new hogsheads, both before and after the lees were first drawn off. The wood was chosen by Latour's own coopers, from the forests of northern Europe around Stettin and Lübeck. The organoleptic qualities of wood of various origins was well-known. Sweet chestnut wood was tart, pine was aromatic but the local oak trees were

only suitable for lesser wines. Lamothe said so explicitly and stored the 1809 Latour in local wood since the wine of that year was not considered good enough for the English market. The use of good quality new wood had no theories to back it up, but the benefits were known to wine-makers and it was considered a worthwhile investment. The cooperage budget accounted for 20 per cent of production costs.

Clarifying the wine with white of egg or albumen, known as *collage à l'œuf*, was practised from the mid-eighteenth century. At the time it was called *fouettage*, or beating, because the operation consisted of beating egg whites, pouring them into the barrel and beating the wine with a whisk. This was done once a year, and if necessary, just before bottling, although wine was never bottled at Latour; it was always sold in hogsheads, which were not returned. The Chartrons wine merchants aged the wines, often resorting to the notorious *coupages* or blends with Ermitage or Spanish wines, but dispatching the wine in hogsheads. In 1786, about one hundred bottles were filled and corked at Latour. In some years, two or three times this number of bottles was produced but the practice was rare, as bottles were expensive and they broke during transit. Moreover, the châteaux wine-makers did not intend to turn themselves into bottlers. The estate managers, however, who recommended long ageing times (six or seven years) in the hogshead, were well aware that after this period wine did not gain anything by being aged in wood, even if the vats were topped up regularly. Lamothe wrote: "there is a limit to storage in the cask, and beyond that time the wine will degenerate if it is not put into glass". Elsewhere, he specifies that "wine is preserved and renewed because it is not subjected to contact with air". These comments were inspired by the Latour of 1807, which was still in the vat by 1815!

The "œnological" knowledge (the adjective did not appear in French until 1823, derived from the noun "œnology", which was adapted from the Greek in the seventeenth century) of the estate managers from 1750 onwards was almost as great as in modern times. If a few details escaped them, it is because they were unimportant, as the following table shows:

1750		LATE 19TH – 20TH CENTURY

. First cabernet,
    followed by Malbec, Petit Verdot
. Best plots
. Filtering soils
. Little or no change
. Ad hoc pruning
. Old vines
. Very dense plantings
. Harvesting neither too early,
    nor too late
. Sorting the harvest
	. Pressing
	. Little or no scraping
	. No need for chaptalisation
	    (first half of nineteenth century)
	. Selection of lands
	    and casks (secondary wine)
	. Drawing off lees
	. Drawing off
	. Egg-white clarification
	. Wood chosen for
	    hogsheads
		. Adding Merlot
		. Complete scrapings
		. Much extraction
		    (strengthenings, long in cask)
		. Heat regulation
		. Controlled malolactic
		    fermentation
		. Shorter ageing
		. High alcoholic content

It should be noted that malolactic fermentation was favoured unwittingly in the past but only when vines were aged for a long time. Since lesser wines were aged for a shorter period, it merely accentuated the difference between the *crus* and other wines. Short vat fermentation (a week in the past, nowadays twenty to thirty days) was no doubt justified by a quest for finesse and the natural concentration of the vines. The questions of yield per hectare and extraction are linked. Nowadays, the yield averages three times the amount produced in the eighteenth century (15.8 hectolitres per hectare). When the yield increases, the maximum must be extracted from the grape. Furthermore, tastes have changed radically and the desired increase in alcoholic content is commensurate with greater extraction. Estate managers in the past were not concerned with the temperature at which fermentation took place and they never mention fermentation being arrested due to too much heat. Temperature regulation appears to have been naturally sufficient for it not to have been a worry. The very long ageing process (more than twice as long as today) proves that despite their short ageing in the vat, the wines were concentrated. From the end of the nineteenth century, wine-producers all over the world reduced the ageing time.

LAMOTHE: EFFICIENCY AND PERSONAL GAIN

Lamothe's skill is unquestioned, but over the years he tended to think of Latour as his personal property, and began to use his time, his manpower and the château's facilities for his own ends. More seriously, Lamothe hid wines from the owners and sold them for his own benefit. It should be stated in his defence that the Ségur heirs hardly ever visited Latour, less than once every ten years, and that all contact with the owners was made by letter. In such circumstances, the owners could hardly have checked the production, equipment and any resulting losses.

The situation could have continued indefinitely but Lamothe became over-confident and did not modify his behaviour when the new co-owners, the Bordeaux wine-merchants who had acquired the *quart Latour*, took over. His carelessness was all the worse since Barton and Guestier also owned and ran the châteaux of Beychevelle and Langoa at Saint-Julien, and Batailley at Pauillac. They were extremely knowledgeable about the costs involved in wine-making and were astonished to discover that the Ségur heirs had not been receiving statements of account for the past nine years. Eventually, another of the co-owners of the *quart Latour*, Dr. Monbalon, exposed the malpractice and pointed out that an estate cannot run itself, since Lamothe was old and living in Bordeaux.

In October 1835, three of the Ségur heirs, Messrs. de Beaumont, de Courtivron and de Fayet visited Latour, something they had never done together before, and dismissed Lamothe. In fact, his death the following month absolved him from having to produce any accounts. His heirs, however, were required to do so in court, and despite the fact that

the books had been badly kept, assessors demonstrated that in twenty-seven years of operations, Lamothe had diverted 207 casks of great wine to his own profit, to which should be added one hundred hogsheads of wine which had disappeared from the Bordeaux wine store. The lawsuit lasted for fourteen years and utterly destroyed the trust the owners had placed in their estate manager.

GUILLAUME-PASCAL TENET: TRANSITION AND VERSATILITY

Guillaume-Pascal Tenet succeeded Lamothe in 1835. As an interim estate manager, he needed to be honest — a vital asset at a time when the owners were uncovering the misdeeds of Lamothe — and skilled, but he appeared to lack the necessary competitive spirit as far as his task of selling the wine was concerned. Nor was his judgement to be relied upon. He twice gave the owners poor advice, causing them to lose two cases against neighbouring landowners, one of them against the Pichon family. This was awkward as the Ségur heirs and the Pichon family moved in the same exalted circles. Furthermore, under Tenet the estate was not earning much, because in 1839 the Ségur heirs needed money to buy the Latour shares in the Monbalon inheritance. Guestier lent them the sum required (FF115,300), but they very much wanted to be free of this financial commitment.

The reunification of the estate in 1841 and the creation of the civil partnership in 1842 marked the end of Lamothe's cavalier – to put it politely – management style. Henceforward, the estate manager became an employee of the partnership and Latour became what in modern parlance would be called a small business. The job of the estate manager became one of controlling expenditure and the owners took a closer interest in the wine sales, because they needed income to be able to repay their loans. The uncertainty involved in forecasting the income from sales of wine has already been mentioned.

That is why Barton and Guestier's offer to contract to buy wine on a regular basis suited the owners, who could then be assured of a regular income. Tenet was consulted in order to determine the average production which could be expected. After much hesitation, he proposed the figure of seventy-five casks, but did not convince the Ségur heirs of his ability to negotiate with Barton and Guestier's representative, Lawton. The contract, eventually signed in June 1844, was for FF1,750 per cask, for both primary and secondary wines, minus a 6 per cent discount. In 1847, Tenet, suspected of having diverted to his own use more than three hundred casks in four years, was replaced by Étienne Benjamin Boutet.

ÉTIENNE-BENJAMIN BOUTET: SKILL AND EFFICIENCY

Before joining Latour, Étienne-Benjamin Boutet had managed Bel-Air for the Marquis d'Aligre. This experience was beneficial in helping to restore the vineyard, which Tenet had neglected. As soon as he arrived, Boutet noted that an additional ninety-five thousand vine stocks were needed, which convinced him to undertake major replanting. The operation was all the more urgent because Tenet had experimented with some extraordinary varieties such as Syrah, although this was logical at a time when the wine merchants were in the habit of stockpiling the great Médocs, as well as white wines, Muscats and Chasselas for long periods. Boutet replanted with Malbec, Cabernet-Sauvignon, Carménère, and even Merlot, which is how this vine stock came to be grown on the estate. When he left Latour in 1855, the property was planted with a suitable mixture of stocks – 56.8% Cabernet-Sauvignon, 22.7% with the two Cabernets (Franc and Sauvignon together), 13.9% Malbec, 5% Merlot and 1.6% Petit Verdot. There were also a number of minor stocks, though the outlandish varieties had been removed.

At the same time, Boutet attacked the drainage problem. He wrote that "water is the greatest enemy of the vine" and noted that the sole drawback of the Latour estate was "the great misfortune of being too wet". This had been known for a long time, with Domenger laying the first drainage pipes. Tenet had also laid some, but these had little effect because they were laid incorrectly and the project had been underfunded. Boutet undertook a considerable amount of work, laying more than 2.5 kilometres of drainage pipes. This repair work resulted in long-term expenditure and thus a reduction in profits

Facing:
The wine store.

from the property. This was all that was needed for minor disputes to arise between Boutet and the directors of the company. Boutet was accused of abusing his position by having his private garden tended to by the Latour gardener, using the Latour horse and carriage, and so on. These peccadillos were probably genuine but Boutet had authority over his staff, was good at restoring and maintaining a vineyard, and his ledgers were in order. In view of the tensions, however, he preferred to resign in 1855, presumably having already secured his future, since soon afterwards he was appointed estate manager of Château Margaux. The contract had expired with the 1853 vintage. Latour had not done well out of the arrangement because there had been three or four exceptional vintages which had fetched very high prices. The resulting loss for the owners was not covered by the six leaner years. Furthermore, the cost of cultivation and overheads (especially a huge increase in the price of oak for the casks) had exceeded forecasts by at least 10 per cent, and there had been a dispute over how much wine the hogsheads held, which was settled by a disbursement of FF10,000 (the equivalent of almost six hogsheads of good wine). Naturally, therefore, the offer to renew the contract was not welcomed, the owners having learnt from experience

that direct management was preferable. Furthermore, some of the shareholders owned other wine-producing properties. The de Beaumonts had vineyards in Touraine, and the Courtivrons in Burgundy. The proposal was rejected and the Bordeaux wine merchants were once again subject to Latour's conditions. A buyer was found for the 1854 vintage at FF5,000 a cask (50 per cent less for the second pressing) and the 1855 vintage sold for FF2,800 (50 per cent for the second pressing), which was far better than the contracted price of FF1,750. Boutet left and was replaced by Justin Roux.

JUSTIN ROUX: ESTATE MANAGER OF THE GOLDEN AGE

Roux was a notary and a former mayor of Pauillac, so he had little in common with his predecessors. He was lucky enough to start work at the beginning of the golden age of Médoc, even though he had to fight to control the first serious disease of the vines, oidium wilt.

Above and opposite: Filling the casks.

The fungus first appeared in 1851, and Boutet had to deal with it from 1852, when it was first found at Latour. Boutet first warned of the danger in 1853. Anything and everything was tried to eradicate it in the Gironde region – spraying with vinegar, soot, soda, etc. Of the various remedies being tried, Boutet chose sulphur, but since the chemical was washed away by the rain, it was ineffectual. He subsequently tried cutting out the infected bunches of grapes, and in 1854 coated the vines with plaster and oil.

Justin Roux had little success stopping the spread of the fungus wilt and was in despair. Although many favoured the use of sulphur, the œnologists complained that the wines were "acquiring the flavour of the sulphur".

The owners were fairly traditionalist and did not like the sulphur sprays, but production continued to decrease. When it dropped to less than half what it had been in 1853, they decided to take action. The Marquis de Beaumont-Villemanzy asserted that the Comte Duchâtel had obtained a normal harvest in those parts of his vineyard at Lagrange (Saint-Julien) which had been treated with sulphur. Furthermore, "his wine never contained even the slightest hint of sulphur". On the other hand, the wine merchant Guestier and the *courtier* Lawton claimed that sulphur tainted the wine. The Marquis de Beaumont and Justin Roux went to Lafite to taste wine from a treated vine and detected no trace of sulphur, but the wine seemed flat to them. In 1858, Justin Roux received permission to test sulphuring on the plot called "La Pinada", which lay outside the estate. The test was not conclusive, although the wine did not smell sulphurous.

In 1861, another serious attack of oidium determined Justin Roux to follow the example of his neighbours, Lascases and Pichon, and he began to treat the vines with sulphur. From 1863, the treatment was increased as a preventive measure. At the same time, Justin Roux continued working to improve draining and laid earthenware drainage pipes for the first time.

All this meant that Latour was in excellent order at the best possible time. A combination of favourable factors came together; the long, slow process of improvement of the vineyard began to bear fruit, and the yield henceforward averaged more than one hundred casks, an increase of more than 70 per cent over the previous ten harvests. In addition,

Opposite: First-year storage.

the selling price of the wine doubled. Under such conditions, the estate manager felt confident in proposing more expenditure. A new wine store was built in 1860, and enlarged in 1875; a dining-room was built for the harvesters, the presses were improved, and so on. It was then that Latour became Château Latour, since the château which still stands in the grounds was finally built (1862-1864). Justin Roux arranged sales, but in close cooperation with the general supervisor, who was one of the owners and who had the final say as to the price to be set or accepted. Roux ensured that the estate was properly run but did not introduce any innovation into cultivation or vinification, although he managed to overcome oidium by sulphuring, the technique finally adopted. In 1857, he registered the Latour trademark with the courts. The wine continued to be sold in hogsheads, but it was bottled sooner, since the taste of buyers and the interests of the wine merchants had reduced the ageing period from six to three years. These same wine merchants now tend to leave the château to do the ageing.

A few wine merchants even entrusted the château with the bottling, under the supervision of the estate manager. At the time (1870), the estate manager was responsible for bottling the wine to be sent to the owners (fourteen hogsheads). The name of the château and the vintage appeared on the corks, and were repeated on the label. The first label to be designed at Latour was for the 1863 vintage and is very similar to the label still in use today.

The opening of the Médoc railway line in 1870 did much to change the way that wines were marketed. Wines which were château-bottled, and thus clearly identifiable, increased the responsibility of the producer, while reducing that of the merchant. This was noted by the owners who were very concerned to maintain the high reputation of Latour, and thus decided not to allow the château's stamp to be used on every bottle. A few minor vintages, even though the wine was bottled at the château, were not stamped at the request of the merchant and at his expense. The ageing Justin Roux could be proud of his work. The estate was running smoothly and it seemed as though nothing could go wrong.

However, the years 1860-1870 brought a new plague to the French vineyards. Phylloxera, which had been reported in the Rhône Valley in 1863, destroyed the vines of the Midi. In 1869, it was found not far from Bordeaux. As had happened in the Rhône Valley, these plant lice had arrived on American vine seedlings which had been imported and planted by two vine-growers, one at Florac, the other at Bouillac.

The owners had learned the lesson from the oidium misfortune and this time took preventive measures. In 1870, they began collecting studies published on the subject. Justin Roux also began to make investigations, but the Marquis de Flers, who advocated carbon sulphate and immersion, believed in prevention rather than cure. In September 1880, vines at Latour were found to be infested with phylloxera. There was universal consternation. A prize of FF300,000 was offered to the inventor of an effective treatment. Naturally, this produced some ridiculous proposals and far-fetched inventions, and there were the inevitable religious processions. For example, the Latour accounts show that in May 1880 twelve days' pay went to men (FF24) and fifteen days' pay to women (FF11.25) for them to take part in an anti-phylloxera procession held on behalf of Latour. Despite these efforts, the plant-louse attacked four months later. In November 1880, a specialist was brought in to treat the Latour vines with carbon sulphate, but treatment had to be repeated several times. At the same time, a preparation called *poudre de Garros* was under consideration for use at Latour. This was an invention by a vine-grower in Bordeaux whom the Comte de Courtivron consulted in the company of Justin Roux (1881). This powder was merely a fertiliser which was tried as a last resort, despite the fact that the owners claimed – and rightly – that fertiliser would spoil the quality of the wine.

Justin Roux did not live to see the result of all his experiments as he passed away in April 1883. He was replaced by Daniel Jouet.

DANIEL JOUET: THE TECHNICIAN AND WINE EXPERT

Jouet was another estate manager who was very different from his predecessors. He was a graduate of the *Institut national agronomique* (National Agronomical Institute) and thus had extensive technical skills. He appears to have been chosen from among numerous candidates,

partly because he was then acting as assistant to the inspector-general of an official body established to combat phylloxera in the Gironde *département*.

The prosperity which Latour enjoyed at the time contributed to the calmness, whether real or assumed, of the owners. "We must wait, without deceiving ourselves but without undue fear, which serves no useful purpose", as the Comte de Courtivron put it. At the time, a huge syringe called a *pal de Gastine*, was being used to inject the vines with carbon sulphate. The parasite was still capable, however, of causing enormous damage. At Entre-Deux-Mers, which had been heavily invaded by phylloxera, several estates lost 90 per cent of their production. Upon arrival, Jouet launched a massive campaign. He stopped the application of the *poudre de Garros*, which he considered to be a piece of charlatanism, and introduced a costly treatment using potassium sulpho-carbonate. This required special equipment consisting of a steam engine and a multitude of pipes. He then formed a special team to fight the pest, the effects of which were still noticeable up to 1916.

The entire vineyard (about five hundred thousand vines) was treated in three years. Each vine received 117 grams of the chemical, a total of over 55 tonnes. Jouet subsequently alternated the potassium sulpho-carbonate treatment with the spreading of carbon sulphate, using a special plough. At the same time, a policy of reconstituting the vineyard

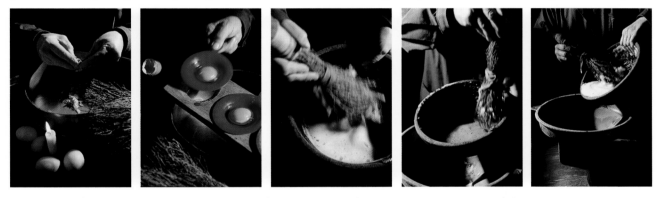

using grafted plants was introduced in 1885. There was some initial hesitation, as it was not certain from the first vintages whether the quality of the wine would suffer. The caution which the technicians displayed saved the great vineyards of Médoc from taking the easy way out, as had been done in the Midi. There, phylloxera-resistant hybrids had been planted immediately, but the wine they produced was coarse and the taste "foxy". Such wines would have ruined the carefully preserved reputations of the *premiers crus*.

At Latour, it was not until the first year of the twentieth century that the complete replanting of the new grafted seedlings was accepted. A Bordeaux university researcher named Millardet carefully hybridised new root-stocks which suited the various types of grafts and soil. The 101-14 and Riparia-gloire, which are used to this day, were of a quality that was high enough to win over the grape-growers.

The list of vine pests would be incomplete without mentioning mildew, another disease imported from the United States on American seedlings, which attacks the leaves and

Above and opposite: Fining: the eggs are broken, the yolks separated, the whites beaten and incorporated into the wine. The resulting emulsion falls to the bottom of the cask, taking with it any impurities suspended in the liquid.

kills the vine. It is through the leaves that the vine fills the grapes with sugar, so the grapes cannot ripen if the diseased leaves cannot feed them. Mildew was discovered in the Rhône Valley in 1878 and in the Gironde region three years later. In 1881, the famous vine-grower, Bellot Des Minières, owner of Haut-Bailly (Graves) — a novel has been written about him — found mildew in his vineyard. It reached Médoc the following year. Measurements showed that half of the sugar was being lost in the grapes and there was an increase in acidity of about 25 per cent. In these circumstances, it is impossible to make a great wine, or even a reasonable one.

Daniel Jouet recognised this fact: "In total, sales for the three years 1885, 1889 and 1891 are insignificant … [The wine should be] sold to a pure-blooded Parisian who is incapable of telling the difference between sour and rancid." This statement was made by one of the finest œnologists of his day, since all the contemporary evidence points to Jouet's taste and discernment. It also implies that the British market could not be duped by having mildewed wines foisted upon it. While a miracle cure was being sought, production dwindled and no money was coming in. The acknowledged poor quality of the wines caused prices to drop. Again, a combination of factors was at work but this time it produced a crisis. Less wine was produced and for a lower price.

*welve days' pay went to men and fifteen days' pay to women to join an anti-phylloxera procession. But this preventive measure did not help Latour, as the plant-louse struck four months later.*

By chance, an unexpected helping hand was received. Professor Millardet, who was visiting Ducru-Beaucaillou (Saint-Julien) in the autumn of 1882, noticed that the vines growing along pathways which had been sprinkled with a blue substance, appeared to be in perfect health. The estate manager, Ernest David, explained that the blue chemical was sprayed on grapes and vines to discourage pilferers, and that it was a powder made of lime mixed with copper sulphate. Ernest David had unwittingly invented Bordeaux mixture. Millardet and Ulysse Gayon studied the active principles in this mixture and after many experiments *in situ* in 1883 and 1884, they found the correct proportions, creating the Bordeaux mixture that is still in use today as a fungicide.

Bordeaux mixture was used at Latour from 1886 onwards. Once again, Daniel Jouet led the fight with customary efficiency, acquired the equipment needed and trained the staff in fighting the deadly fungus. There were now effective measures to control oidium, mildew and phylloxera. Carbon sulphate was widely used, as was iron sulphate to combat vine-rust, a new disease which attacked the wood (1882). The vine-grower's medicine chest also contained an insecticide for use against the flea-beetle, a pest which had been

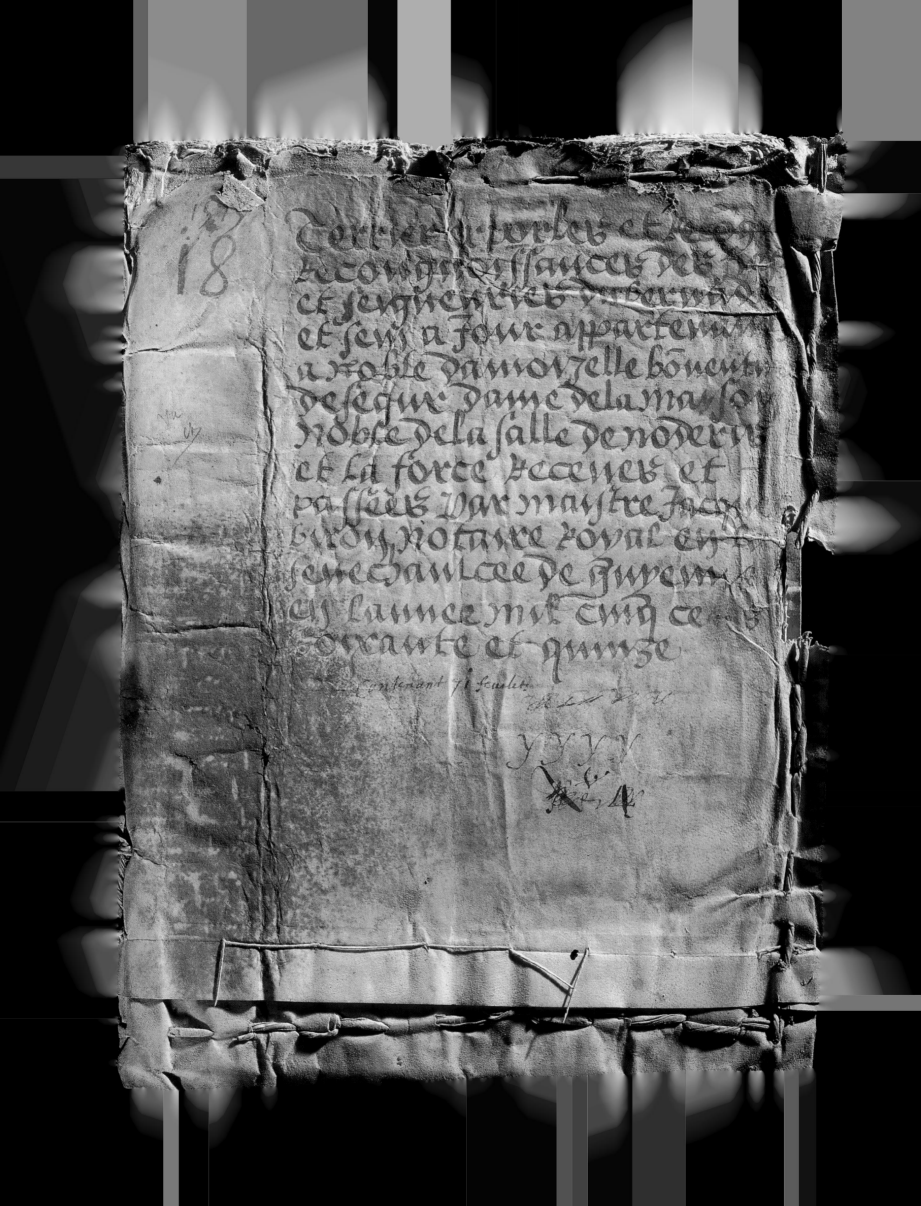

18

Terrier a porter et baulx
recognoissances des (...)
et servitentes (...)
et cens a eulx appartenans
a noble damoizelle bonneventur
de seguir dame de la maison
noble de la salle de noferin
et la force secener et
passées par maistre (...)
birdu notaire royal en
seneschaucee de Auvergne
(...) l'annee mil cinq cens
soixante et quinze

Contenant 71 feuillets

XXV

GRAND VIN
DE LATOUR

present in Médoc since at least the seventeenth century. Later scourges included the eudemis moth, cochylis worm, the root-rot fungus and even the cochineal beetle. The estate manager had his work cut out for him, protecting the vine and fighting its enemies at great expense. The defence of a *premier cru* could not be neglected, even if the budget suffered. In fact, it suffered to such an extent that the *Société civile du vignoble de Latour* found itself in debt again and had to borrow money in 1886, 1889, 1892, 1896, and so on.

VINES AND WINES AFTER THE VICTORY

The struggle against these crop diseases had numerous economic, social and technological consequences (for agriculture and vinification) and there were even moral lessons to be learned. For instance, as soon as phylloxera was discovered, the area to be manured needed to be greatly increased, and in 1880, under Justin Roux, manuring was extended from 225 to 475 cubic metres. The aim was to make the vines as healthy as possible to enable them to resist both the attacks of various pests and the "shock treatments" which were necessary.

Contrary to what one might think and to what has been written, the phylloxera and mildew years produced abundant harvest. There was an increase of more than 30 percent with the advent of Jouet, a professional agronomist. The volume of manure spread was again increased, eventually attaining an annual average of 1,245 cubic metres, and its effects were combined with those of the early artificial fertilisers.

Diseases of the vine did much to change traditional customs. When the contract for wine purchase was signed in 1844, it was stipulated that only one-twentieth of the vineyard was to be manured, hardly more than was required for replanting purposes. At the height of the battle against diseases of the vine, the owners did all they could to help the estate manager win; but as soon as the threat was lifted, some of them began to worry about "unnecessary procedures". In 1895, the Marquis de Flers declared that he did not want to "sacrifice quality to increase quantity". His words echoed the concerns expressed by the wine merchants, who had already noted the reduction in quality, which had produced a much lower selling price for the wine.

Prior to 1880, the contracts for buying wine never mentioned yield per hectare, all that was stipulated was that manuring should be limited to one-twentieth and replanting restricted to one-fortieth. Later contracts required production to be limited as, over and above a certain quota, the purchase price would drop. The estate manager maintained, however, the right to vinify in any way he saw fit.

In the person of Daniel Jouet, Latour progressed from empiricism to technical expertise; he could be described as an early œnologist, since he frequently consulted Ulysse Gayon, founder of the Bordeaux Œnology Laboratory. Henceforward, the policy of wine-making

was based on measurement and analysis, and not merely on impression, instinct and whatever was visible to the naked eye. Until the advent of the vine diseases, redressing the balance was left to "Nature" in normal years. As soon as it was learned that the soil could be manipulated, the consequences were taken into account and scientific methods were adopted to do so, using the appropriate additives.

In 1883, Jouet purchased a glucometer in order to be able to gauge the sugar content in a grape (when vines were forced, the sugar content dropped). Shortly thereafter, in the same vein, the wine merchants wanted to know what they were buying and subjected the wines to bacteriological examination, and tests of alcoholic content. This new attitude emerged with the advent of the twentieth century. Before fertilisation, the alcohol content of the wine was of no interest and the archives never mention it. From the year 1900, Jouet vinified the wine using an alcoholometer and a temperature gauge. The part played by temperature in fermentation, which was unknown until then, started to be taken into account. For instance, in 1906 – a great year – the temperature in the casks was 31°C, that is to say the temperature considered desirable today.

There is a serious inherent risk, as fermentation is known to stop at just a few degrees higher. Daniel Jouet thus decided to cool the casks if they overheated, using blocks of ice ordered from Bordeaux. The manufacturer made a fortune delivering his ice to the châteaux. It is difficult to determine the date on which ice was first used at Latour, but it was probably just before 1906, when it is certain that Jouet cooled a few casks.

The "weighing" of musts, the measuring of their alcoholic proof and the high yields resulted in the use of chaptalisation, which wine merchants advocated and to which the owners put up a weak resistance. Adding sugar to the wine did not trouble them much, it was the cost of the operation which they were against. As we know, Lamothe chaptalised the 1816 vintage, but did not greatly benefit from it, probably because he had added too little sugar.

Starting with the 1908, 1909 and 1910 vintages, at the request of the wine merchants who had bought the wine under contract, chaptalisation was carried out. The owners thus had no need to worry about poor sales. Jouet agreed to chaptalise and later wrote: "Our chaptalisation operation has been a huge success. It is a real lesson for the future." Consequently, even when the contract ended, Jouet did not forget the experiment.

He did not chaptalise in 1911, because the vintage was a good one, but in 1912, when the Cabernets-Sauvignons only averaged 11° proof, he chaptalised a little on his own authority. After all, the estate manager is the only judge of the vinification process. Between the late nineteenth and early twentieth century, Daniel Jouet still did not scrape the grapes but he left the wine to ferment in the vats for a long time. He thus moved away from the methods used half a century earlier, when the wine was sometimes drawn off without waiting for alcoholic fermentation to be completed. Jouet wanted the opposite to happen – for the wine to clarify in the vat. Drawing off the wine is not a simple operation because the wine from each vat needs to be divided equally between each of the hogsheads so that it will age uniformly. The vats are tapped and the wine is poured into a pitcher from  which it is poured by hand into the hogshead. Indeed, there was no other option, as industrial electricity did not reach Latour until 1931.

The next stage involved an alchemy, the secret of which was known only to the estate manager, and which is called *égalisage*, or equalling. The operation consisted in assembling various wines – great wines, second pressing and subsequent pressings – to obtain the best quality and the definitive great wines and secondary wines. Daniel Jouet, who was a brilliant wine-taster, excelled at this and kept the owners fully informed. They were deeply interested in the operation, which would determine how much the estate would earn. A new tendency emerged, that of mixing the best second pressing with the great wine, which was seasoned with a little wine from later pressings, while wine from the later pressings was incorporated into the secondary wine along with some lee wine from a previous vintage. This use to which previous vintages was put is not surprising. Some wines are slow to mature and cannot be used too soon. This is especially the case with wines whose lees need to be decanted, or wines from pressing which need to be fined. Today, thanks to a system known as a "pressing bank", numerous wine-makers incorporate "pressings" from previous years into the latest vintage.

After much hesitation, the side bung system was adopted in the winery for second-year storage. At the end of the third year of ageing, the wine was supplied in hogsheads or bottled for the owners or wine merchants, always on the responsibility of the estate manager.

An important innovation appeared in the vineyard, which gave the vines the look they have today. This was the training of vines along wires, a method decided upon by Daniel Jouet as

soon as he was appointed. Although this method of training vines was an old invention, the recent industrial production of wire made it financially viable. It replaced the wooden strips joined to wooden pickets. This was better for the health of the vine because the problems caused by the wood rotting were eliminated, the vines were easier to care for and the running costs consequently reduced. But to train all the Latour vines over wires took almost forty years.

The increase in production resulted in an increase in the unsold balance of wines from later pressings or excess wine which could not be used in secondary wines. Up until now, such wines, which were sometimes reserved for topping up, had been returned to the owners or sold to friends, but the volume was such that it inspired the idea of launching a second trademark which might generate additional profits. This was what Lafite had done with its Carruades, and Château Margaux with its Pavillon-Margaux. Thus in 1907 the "wines of Saint-Lambert" trademark was born, for which Daniel Jouet created selections and blends of secondary wines and wines of later pressings. He advised against the Saint-Lambert wines having vintages, so that he could have more freedom to blend them. The new wine produced about forty hogsheads a year and brought in additional income of about ten thousand francs, which was particularly welcome because the partnership was not doing particularly well, despite its successful fight against diseases of the vineyard.

For a number of years, the owners did not draw a dividend, running costs increased and social unrest mounted until the outbreak of war in 1914. Daniel Jouet, loyal to his post, submitted regular reports to the owners, whose military commitments prevented them from visiting the estate. The mildew, of which traces still remained, had left unpleasant memories in the minds of wine merchants and customers. Mildewed wines either did not age, or aged badly. The reputation of the great clarets, which had remained intact and had been fiercely defended for two centuries, had been undermined. This disaster forced the *premiers crus* estates of the Bordeaux region to establish ties and in 1924 they took an important decision: they would bottle their wines on their estates. This was all the more important as wines under false or forged labels had been on the market for some time. In 1926 an underground wine store was built at Latour so that in the future

Opposite: A set of labels for the magnificent 1990 vintage.

GRAND VIN
DE
CHATEAU LATOUR
PREMIER GRAND CRU CLASSÉ
PAUILLAC
1990
Alc. 12,5 % Vol.
DÉPOSÉ
APPELLATION PAUILLAC CONTROLÉE
STÉ CIVILE DU VIGNOBLE DE CHATEAU LATOUR, PROPRIÉTAIRE A

all the wine could be aged for three years on the estate. This was the final innovation of the "Jouet reign". The now elderly estate manager resigned in 1932, and was replaced by Pierre Brugière, the agronomist who had been his assistant for four years.

PIERRE BRUGIÈRE: WISE AND LOYAL

This new estate manager scrupulously followed in Daniel Jouet's footsteps. He had had the same training and plenty of experience, having been the estate manager of the Château Beychevelle. The tasks of an estate manager no longer allowed room for improvisation or experimentation. Financial restrictions and the dictates of œnology laid down a very clear course of action, even when the general circumstances were adverse. The Wall Street Crash of 1929 hit Europe, minor vintages succeeded each other without causing much stir, and new social problems made trading conditions difficult. Threats of war, followed by war itself, brought additional problems. The limited financial resources available to the estate forced the estate manager to act cautiously and unambitiously.

When prosperity finally returned in 1952, it was not accompanied by any new dynamism. One cannot second-guess a market which one regards with caution. Production had been increasing since 1949, requiring the purchase of two new wine-presses and an increase in storage space. Further storage was needed in 1962, when production reached unimaginable heights. In 1963, when the Ségur heirs sold Latour, Pierre Brugière did not want to join the new team after working on the estate for thirty-one years. He went into retirement, and died fifteen years later. The new board of directors, chaired by David L. Pollock, appointed two successors with the status of joint managers, Henri Martin and Jean-Paul Gardère.

HENRI MARTIN – JEAN-PAUL GARDÈRE: THE INNOVATORS

Henri Martin had been the mayor of Saint-Julien for decades. He was also the creator of Château Gloria, one of the best bourgeois *crus* of its day. He had demonstrated his skill in four areas: tending the vines, vinification, sales and publicity. Jean-Paul Gardère, meanwhile, was a self-made man. At the age of forty-three, he had his own wine brokerage firm and published a newsletter on wine and wine sales. He knew the world of wine extremely well. This duo set about the badly needed modernisation of Latour. The former owners and most recent estate managers had, of course, kept the vineyard in good condition, but the conservatism of the owners, the fact that Brugière was elderly, and over-thrifty management had meant that the "tools of production" had not been modernised in any way. In 1962-1963, tractors and cultivators were being used in almost every other vineyard, but at Latour draught animals were still the norm. Henri Martin and Jean-Paul Gardère

Following pages: Putting the bottles into cases.

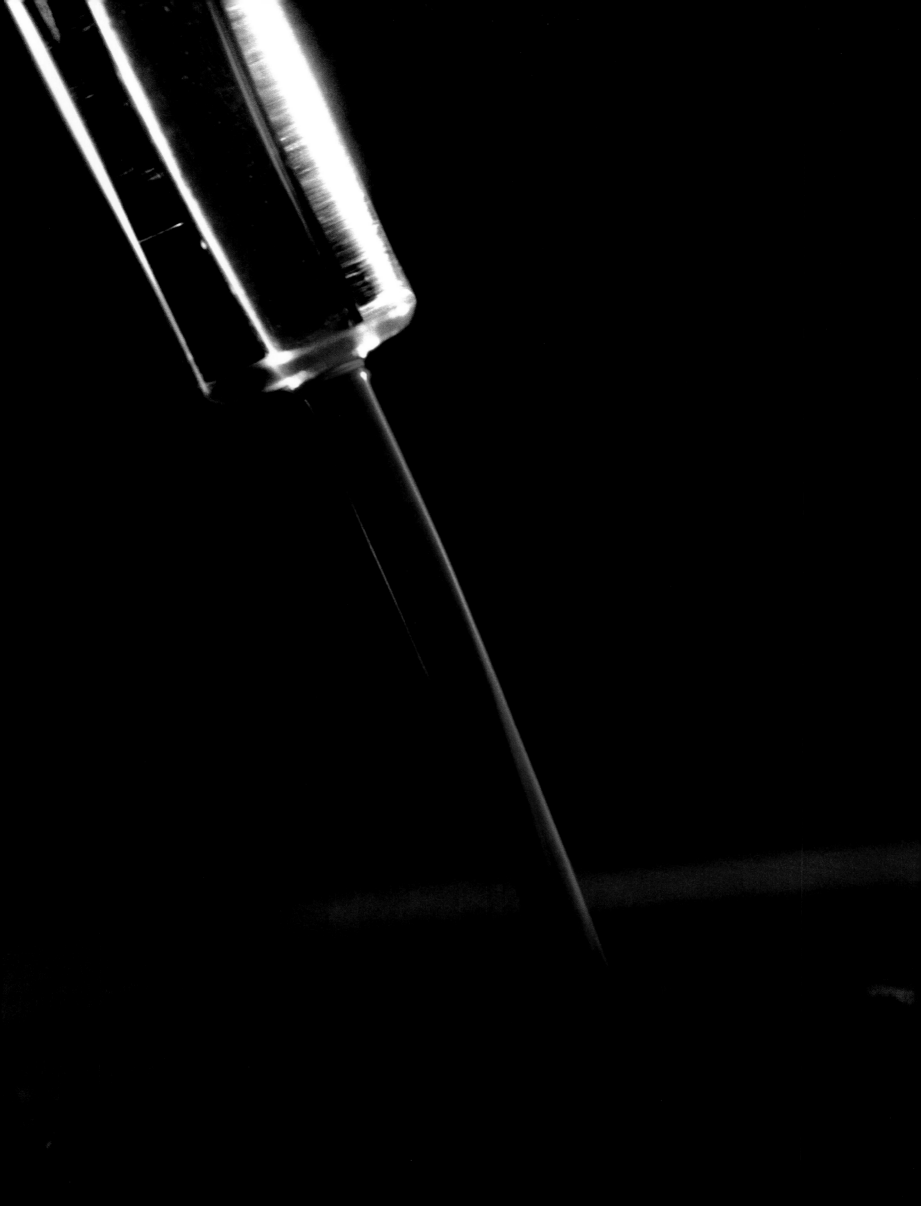

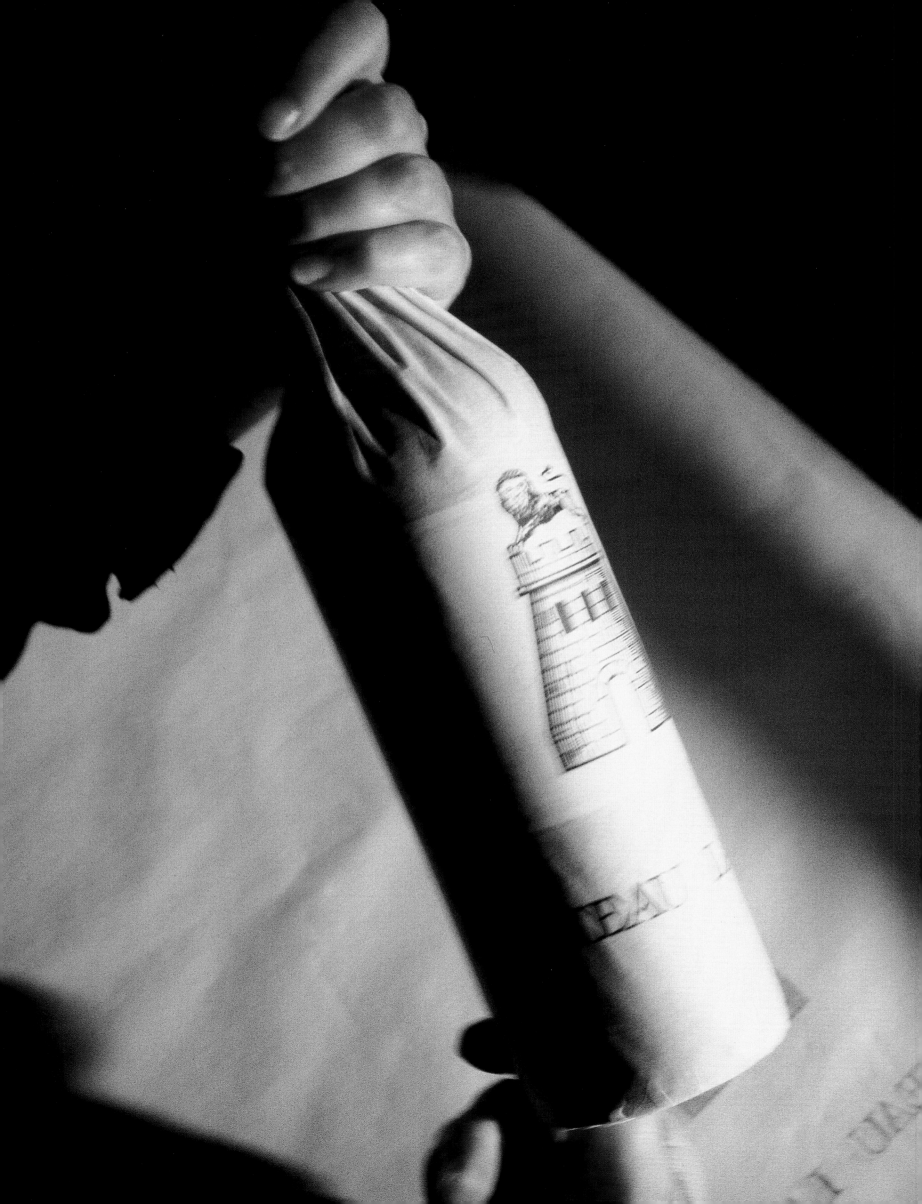

had to work hard to move beyond the limitations of a venerable but over-rigid tradition in order to modernise the equipment and the way the estate was managed, while taking care not to damage the image of the wine. Within a few years, Latour had progressed from the horse to the helicopter, to mechanisation of the scraping process, and so on. From the 1964 vintage onwards, the must fermented in twelve stainless steel vats, each holding 200 hectolitres, which were cooled by spraying. This innovation caused a great stir, which was hardly justified because wine on the estate of La Mission Haut-Brion had been vinified since 1926 in enamelled steel casks. But stainless steel had yet to gain ground in the Médoc region.

At the same time, planting and replanting was undertaken since the vineyard was in

need of a considerable number of vines, but without reducing the age of the vineyard as it was essential to maintain the quality of the great wine. This apparently impossible task was achieved in the following way: rather than replanting the vines plot by plot, young ones were planted beside the old over the whole vineyard. This meant that a double harvest was necessary: that of the old vines (those over thirty-five years old), which would be used for the great wine, and that of the young vines, which would be used in the secondary (or tertiary) wine.

In 1963, the 2.5 hectares of La Pinada were planted and replanted. Its wine was still not counted as "Château Latour". Shortly thereafter, 10 hectares of fallow land on the Bages plateau were planted with vines, although the wine it produced in subsequent years was not incorporated into the great wine. Drainage pipes were renovated, and new and better-designed ones added to get rid of the muddy clay pools whose lack of permeability was choking the vines. This the type of maintenance operation at Latour which the various estate managers had been performing for the past two centuries.

The new plantings, young vines and generous yields led to the idea of producing another wine under a new trademark. It was Henri Martin who suggested using the name from one of the best areas of the vineyard: "*les forts*" de Latour. Latour could not be allowed to produce a commonplace wine, however, and the board of directors imposed certain conditions. The quality was required to meet the criteria for a second *cru*, and the wine should

Opposite: The final operations before the bottles are packed into their cases.

151

be sold "ready to drink", and thus aged in bottles at Latour. The first wine labelled "Forts de Latour" was the 1966 vintage, which was not put on sale until 1971. The goal of achieving the quality of a second *cru* had been attained, if the prices which Forts de Latour commanded at auction are to be believed.

Once again, Latour was in a promising position at the dawn of a new golden age. The yields of 15 or 20 hectolitres per hectare were forgotten, the average now being about 50 hectolitres. At the same time, the price per cask had increased by 500 per cent to reach an average of FF200,000 and an astonishing FF500,000 in 1998.

Volume and price both had cumulative effects and Latour rediscovered the prosperity it had enjoyed between 1850 and 1880. In June 1973, Lord Cowdray, of the Pearson Group, left the board of directors and was replaced by Henri Martin. Six years later, Henri Martin resigned as financial director but remained a board member.

When the civil partnership restructured, Jean-Paul Gardère was appointed estate director. He held this post for three years and resigned after spending twenty years working at Latour. Nevertheless, he remained a board member until 1983, when his colleague, Jean-Louis Mandrau took the title of technical director. But he did not remain long because he was asked to join his family's Entre-Deux-Mers vineyard in the spring of 1986. He was succeeded by Christian Le Sommer, a local man who had worked at Yquem.

CHRISTIAN LE SOMMER: CONTINUITY

In 1986, circumstances forced Latour to harvest unripe grapes for the first time, but this still yielded more than two hundred and fifty casks. In 1989, Allied-Lyons, who held a quarter of the shares, took over the whole estate. For the first time in two centuries, the new chairman of the board, David Orr, who succeeded Alan Hare (1983-1989), was a "wine man", in this case a wine trade specialist.

Christian Le Sommer was the permanent fixture at Latour. The sales manager, John Kolasa, left Latour for Rauzan Sègla in 1994, and was succeeded by Frédéric Engerer. The head grower, Guy Faure, was succeeded by Frédéric Ardouin. The owners changed too. In 1993, Allied-Lyons sold out to François Pinault. The estate director, Christian Le Sommer, has thus ensured continuity; despite his youth, he has become the most senior member of the Latour management team.

CHÂTEAU LATOUR

OR

THE AURA OF A PREMIER CRU

hen the story was told in the first chapter of how Denis de Mullet created a vineyard in the early seventeenth century, it was stated that he selected the land he bought on the basis of rigorous criteria. He had owned the fiefdom of Montguyon, which covered a large part of the "Mayne de La Tor", since 1612 and it was this same "Mayne de La Tor" which he devoted to the monoculture of the vine. It had been observed as early as 1400 that the wine of La Tour (probably from Bourdieu de la Tour) was the best in the vicinity; by 1600, this judgement had been confirmed by the product of two hundred harvests. A cluster of empirical observations had thus inspired a first typology of land suitable for growing wine grapes, in the same way that any farmer knows from experience, but is unable to explain, why a certain crop "grows better here than anywhere else".

The land of Château Latour, so prized because the number of terrains capable of producing *premiers crus* is so extremely limited, has naturally been studied intensively. The climatological and geological factors which influence the growth and fruiting of the vine have been researched, measured and evaluated.

CLIMATOLOGY

Contrary to received wisdom, it is not the warmest and sunniest climes which produce the best grapes, or rather the best wines. In fact, there is a simple rule regarding the optimal climate for the production of fine wines: the vine must be grown at the northern limit of the area in which the grape can ripen fully. Not all varieties of vine need the same amount of heat for their grapes to mature. The Grenache or Carignan varieties would never ripen in the Médoc, but the Cabernets, Merlot and Petit Verdot will ripen perfectly eight or nine years out of ten.

The second rule is as follows: the climate must be even, though small variations are allowed. The climate of the Médoc is a maritime one, warmed and tempered by the Gulf Stream, although there is a noticeable difference between day and night-time temperatures, another requirement if the vine is to develop well.

Furthermore, as with all vineyards, a great vintage is also based on very warm days (30°C) in late summer and no rain during harvesting. In the earlier seasons of the year, and of course during flowering, neither heavy rain nor excessive cold is desirable, and even warm rain is to be avoided as it can cause the grapes to rot. Hail and long cold spells are also damaging.

The Médoc, and especially the Château Latour climate, fulfils all these conditions. However, it cannot be denied that the production of quality wines on the basis of this first rule of climatic conditions involves taking considerable risks, and this is where the dramatic difference lies between one year's vintage and the next.

In this general context, three additional attributes apply to the Château Latour vineyard. Due to its proximity to the Gironde estuary, it is well protected against frost, this being the case even during the terrible winter of 1956; for the same reason, it rarely suffers from hail; and finally, it is very resistant to the bad weather conditions which cause "poor vintages". It is the special soil of the Château Latour vineyard which is responsible for this phenomenon.

THE SOIL

One cannot talk of the Médoc region without mentioning its famous "gravelly outcrops". Not a single *cru* grows on any other type of soil, whether a *premier cru* or lesser one. When these outcrops and gravels are examined closely, they are seen to have other special features. Their effect on the vine also depends on the composition of the soil and the sub-soil, to a depth of 80 centimetres, and this combination is what makes the Latour soil so special. First of all, the gravel stones of the Médoc are the largest in the region. The only similar gravel is in the extreme eastern end of the Lafite vineyard, the other Lafite gravels being much smaller, like those of Mouton Rothschild, the Margaux gravelstones being smaller still. In fact, the swathe of large gravel stones runs parallel to the course of the Gironde; they can thus be found in the vineyards of Ducru-Beaucaillou and Montrose, which are situated on slopes leading down to the river.

Secondly, there is that essential ingredient the sub-soil, where that the vine stocks put out their roots. At Latour it is not calcareous, as at Château Margaux, nor a mixture of gravel and sand, as at Lafite and at Mouton; it is a mixture of clay and marl.

The Latour soil is thus a unique and contrasting combination of an extremely poor, coarse gravel on top of a relatively rich sub-soil. This means that the vines are equipped to fight against two calamities which may befall them in bad years: heavy rains, since the soil drains very well thanks to the gravel; and drought whose effects are mitigated by the richness of the sub-soil.

It should be added that man has done much to improve the almost perfect work of nature. This exceptional soil had only two defects, long identified by the estate managers. These are the presence of muddy patches caused by vertical seams of clay which come to the surface and poor drainage in certain spots.

A million years ago, gravel was brought to the Médoc (including Latour) as a result of the Günz glaciation. Prior to the marine transgression of the Netherlands (4,000 BC), the gravel of the future Château Latour estate had perfect drainage and covered a much larger area, sloping down to where the Gironde now runs, the estuary level being at least twenty metres lower than its current position. When the water level rose, it produced clay deposits and the heavy, muddy clay soil that borders the Gironde and which, at Latour, has been turned into a large water-meadow, separating the vineyard from the estuary.

There was another consequence of the rise in the water level and the emergence of the patches of clay which removed the excellent gravel slopes. It was the formation of fairly deep "sinks" or depressions in the ground which were difficult to drain. For the past two centuries, the estate managers have laid drainage pipes in order to compensate for these inconsistencies of nature, and the muddy patches have been worked hard so that this unique piece of land could become as exceptional as the unique wines it produces.

THE STORY OF THE VINTAGES

The first mention of what was to be Château Latour wine came in 1389. The source was Jean de Treulo, a Bordeaux wine merchant who was for a short time to become the owner of a small share in the manor of Saint-Maubert. Unfortunately, the contract in which the name is mentioned is not very explicit and would disappoint wine connoisseurs. It stipulated that the wine must be "good, pure, clear", delivered in new, non-returnable hogsheads, and that all the wine must come from the Saint-Maubert vineyard owned by Amadieu de la Motte, co-seigneur of La Tour. It can be assumed with certainty that this was a red wine, because Jean de Treulo traded with England, and the English preferred to buy red wine. The word "clear" (*clair*) should be understood in the sense of *clairet*, "claret", the best Bordeaux wine which was destined for the English market.

Much later, in 1638, the wine of La Tour was being sold in a Bordeaux tavern, whose landlord went to La Tour, at the request of Denis de Mullet, to supervise the transport of the wine. This story indicates that the wine, which unfortunately no one had yet thought to describe in any detail, was no ordinary wine since it involved what was almost certainly a long and arduous journey for the publican. It was not until 1663 that the first

comment was made on its quality, and even this was a brief one: "A good flavour, the most particular that I have ever encountered" (Samuel Pepys, writing about the wine of Haut-Brion).

In the fifteenth century, trading was put on a firmer footing. The biggest customers for the great wines, that is to say the expensive wines, were the English. Many Anglo-Irish wine merchants settled in Bordeaux, the main export centre, where Dutch wine merchants specialising in less costly wines had also established a base. Throughout the sixteenth and seventeenth centuries, and until the end of the reign of Louis XIV, the price of wine was heavily dependent on the political and military climate (blockades and boycotts, naval wars, imposition of heavy excise duties, etc.). It was not until 1712 that the trade truly began to flourish.

In 1714, there is the first mention of a wine of Latour under that name, and its price of 450 livres a hogshead, a huge sum. The transaction was performed under the administration of Alexandre de Ségur, who also owned Lafite, where his son, Nicolas-Alexandre, had his country house. Mention has already been made of the period when Lafite and Latour were sold at the same price and by the same "sales force" until the matter of the inheritance of the "Prince of the Vines" was settled in 1761. It was then specified that the 1760 vintage, stored in hogsheads at Latour, would be sold by the Ségur heirs at the same price as the Lafite wine of the same year.

We know the approximate value and quantity of each vintage since 1735, thanks to the rigorous principles of administration of Alexandre de Ségur and his successors. The following figures refer only to the fine wines. The volume of secondary wines produced is on average one-third of the great wine.

Year	Number of Casks	Price per Cask in livres	Comment
1735	40	135	Poor, uninteresting vintage.
1736	48	260	Average year but better than the previous one. N.-A. de Ségur could have sold the wine for more, but he rejected some good offers and wasted a lot of time.
1737	75	300	Poor vintage.
1738	41	1,600	A very great wine.
1739	33	1,600	A great wine, not quite as good as in 1738.
1740	53	180	Uninteresting vintage.
1741	42	1,700	A complete great wine.
1742	60	240	A good wine, which sold very badly, since the English were unable to buy it due to the war.
1743	67	850	Sold very well, although a much thinner wine than 1742.
1744	39	1,400	A great wine.

Year	Number of Casks	Price per Cask in livres	Comment
1745-1749			An average wine, average price.
1749-1750		1,900	
1751		300	A very poor vintage.
1752		1,400	
1753		1,600	
1754		500	This price does not reflect the quality of the wine, which was only slightly inferior to the previous vintage. The English could not buy it.
1755			Death of Chief Justice Ségur and problems of succession.
1757		1,300	
1760			Sixty casks were sold at the same price as those of Lafite. After the next vintage, the two estates were independent of each other. There followed a period of reorganisation at Latour, with the arrival of the estate manager Domenger.
1775	50		A little wine.
1776	40		A little wine.
1777	8		Probably the smallest harvest at Latour, due to damage caused by frost and hail.
1778	44		
1779	58		
1780	66		A little wine.
1781	85		
1782	80		
1783	70		
1784	66	1,300	
1785	104	1,100	A huge harvest, totalling 154 casks
1786	102	1,300	A huge harvest, totalling 152 casks.
1787	45	1,300	A good price for a wine of which it was said that it had "neither body nor consistency".
1788	91	1,400	An average wine. The bitterly cold winter of 1788-1789 caused damage, even at Latour, though here it was less than in other vineyards.
1789	46	600	The wine was of such poor quality that it could not be sold on the English market. The price collapsed. The vintage was still of some interest because Domenger chose three wines (46, 28 and 4.5 casks), on the basis of a formula which was adopted again in the 1970s.
1790	32	2,000	A very good wine.
1791	28	2,200	A very good price for a wine which the estate manager said "had a scalded taste".
1792	32	1,400	A very average wine.
1793	29	1,300	A little wine, the result of late harvesting in October.
1794		2,400	Average wine, hardly better than the two previous ones.
1795		2,200 to 2,400	A truly great wine, which would have fetched a very high price, had the market not succumbed to political events. Probably the best year in the century.

Year	Number of Casks	Price per Cask in livres/FF	Comment
1796	33	1,400 livres	Another little wine following an October harvest.
1797		600 livres	A few hogsheads were sold at 1,500 livres. Very low average price, which bears no relation to the quality of the wine.
1798	58	2,400 livres	Record price beaten only by that of 1795, the other great year of the decade. A very great complete wine, probably the best ever produced by Latour. The harvest began on 17 September.
1799	29	1,000 livres	Rather poor wine, the result of October harvesting.
1800			Wine hardly better than 1799.
1801	69	FF2,400	The price of a very great wine. Again the harvest began on 17 September.
1802	74	FF2,400	Latour had a double triumph (harvest on 22 September). The wine was rounded, smooth and fruity. Considered better than 1801.
1803-1804		FF1,200 to 1,300	Two mediocre vintages. Wines bitter and acid.
1805			Good fruity vintage.
1806		FF750	Weak and acid wine without body.
1807		FF2,400	This must have been the first sale by the new estate manager, Lamothe. A much higher price than the quality deserved, although it was better than the mediocre 1806.
1808	120		Very mediocre wine, flat and green, hardly better than that of 1806.
1809		FF150	An October harvest in rainy weather; one of the worst wines from the estate, green and weak.
1810		FF1,000	Average wine.
1811	74	FF800 to 900	A smooth and fruity wine, sold badly. Very good vintage.
1812	95	FF1,200	Good, but not as good as 1811.
1813	145	FF2,600	These prices seem far too high for a wine lacking concentration.
1814	62	FF3,000	Wine unsuitable for keeping.
1815		FF3,000	Hard to understand why the price paid was the same as for the previous year, when this was a very great wine, rounded, smooth and fruity.
1816	30	FF550	A very little wine, from a rainy October harvest. Of historic interest because it was the first Latour wine to be lightly chaptalised.
1817	Less than 130		A very small harvest due to frost. Not harvested until 5 October. Light wine, transparent body.
1818		FF3,350	The highest price for a great wine, the best since 1802, but stronger and with good keeping qualities.
1819	60	FF3,100	Good price for a wine without much body.
1820	About 25		Small harvest for a fruity wine, clearly better than the previous one.
1821	More than 65	FF1,275	Wine with less body than that of 1820, the result of an October harvest.
1822	90	FF2,600	Full and complete wine, resulting from an extraordinarily early harvest on 28 August.

Year	Number of Casks	Price per Cask in FF	Comment
1823	50 to 60	1,500	Little wine from late harvesting on 6 October.
1824	24		Very small harvest.
1825	About 50	3,350	A record price. Great vinous wine, full, opulent, but to the detriment of finesse.
1826	88	2,000	Average wine, sold quite well.
1827	100	1,700	Another poor year.
1828	65	1,100	Very light wine which was not worth more.
1829	75	1,000	Fourth year of vintage from grapes inadequately ripened. The 1829 was truly mediocre. Furthermore, the hard winter of 1829-1830 destroyed some of the vines of the Médoc and even Latour was not spared.
1830	12	750	The smallest harvest since 1777, due to frost and run-off.
1831	30	2,500	Small harvest due to frost of previous year but good fruity wines. These wines could not match 1825, but were a great improvement on a bad series.
1832	52	1,900	Acceptable quality.
1833	94	1,750	A little wine.
1834	63	2,400	Good wines but rather light and poor keeping qualities.
1835	94	1,700	
1836	83	1,800	
1837	75	2,000	
1838	50	2,200	Poor vintage, difficult to sell.
1839	45	1,400	Little wine of no interest.
1840	85	1,800	The quality of the wine fully justified the much higher price than 1839.
1841	75	1,800	A good wine.
1842	63	1,500	Poor vintage difficult to sell, of average value.
1843	25	1,000	Mediocre wine.
1844	62		A very great wine, fruity and balanced.
1844-1853		Ten-year contract at FF1,750	
1845	53		A thin, acid wine.
1846	65		A great wine, rich and powerful.
1847	75		Light and green.
1848	70		Smooth, good quality.
1849	60		Hard and devoid of charm.
1850	80		A little wine.
1851	75		
1852	90		Light, without body, fairly balanced.
1853	48		Very little wine, thin and acid. (End of the contract.)
1854	13	5,000	Great, complete wine.

Year	Number of Casks	Price per Cask in FF	Comment
1855	35	2,800	Insufficiently mature, just below average.
1856	31	5,000	A high price to pay for a quality hardly better than the previous year.
1857	49	4,400	Fine elegant wine (sunny harvest on 22 September).
1858	111	4,800	Average maturity and body but good (harvest on 22 September).
1859	41	2,750	Hard and graceless (run-off and hail).
1860	109	500	Green, washed out.
1861	87	5,000	Full-bodied, low acidity, mature, good, keeps averagely.
1862	82	4,000	Lively and full-bodied, excellent.
1863	74	2,000	Average.
1864	115	4,500	Full-bodied, smooth, good keeping qualities (harvest on 22 September).
1865	126	5,600	Very successful.
1866	109	700	Rainy harvest on 25 September. Light, fragile, mediocre, unpromising.
1867	74	1,200	Fine but light.
1868	99	6,250	Sunny harvest on 10 September. Excellent, elegant, robust. Record price.
1869	125	3,200	Lack of concentration, thin.
1870	128	3,000	Similar to the previous year.
1871	123	1,800	Very light, acid wine.
1872	113	1,200	Very light, acid wine.
1873	94	2,250	Early October harvest, light, thin, acid.
1874	190	5,500	Lively, elegant, successful (harvest on 18 September).
1875	165	4,000	Harvest on 24 September. A fine wine.
1876	62	2,400	Early October harvest. Little, rather washed out wine.
1877	154	2,600	Mediocre wine.
1878	133	4,000	Late September harvest. Full-bodied, complete wine.
1879	67	2,500	Similar to 1877, a little, green wine.
1880	63	3,800	Weak wine, lacking in body.
1881	69	5,100	Great concentrated wine, good keeping qualities.
1882	42	3,000	Little wine.
1883	68	2,500	Green, washed out wine.
1884	60	3,100	Good, but no more than that (first effect of mildew).
1885	50	3,000	Similar to the previous one (mildew effect still present).
1886	60	3,000	Liquid, a little green.
1887	80	3,000	More vinous than the previous two.
1888	188	2,250	Good wine.
1889	152	3,000	Good wine.
1890	123	4,100	Complete wine (no mildew).
1891	140	2,025	Average quality, not much body, slightly acid.

Year	Number of Casks	Price per Cask in FF	Comment
1892	120	110	Grapes not very ripe, lack of body.
1893	177	1,750	Great, full-bodied wine. Harvested on 20 August.
1894	70	1,250	October harvest in the rain. Watery, uninteresting wine (mildew).
1895	90	425 to 450	Declassified vintage ("red wine from Pauillac"), very little wine.
1896	190	1,500	Light, unambitious wine.
1897	87	700	Rain and disease. Declassified. Similar to 1895.
1898	90	1,625	Late September harvest. No disease, excellent, balanced wine.
1899	130	2,000	Great wine, elegant and complete.
1900	200	1,160	Huge harvest, no concentration, a light wine.
1901	215	780	Cold and wet. Oidium, mildew. Thin and colourless.
1902	170	880	Cold and wet. Oidium, mildew. Thin and colourless.
1903	165	1,000	Cold and wet. Not much better than the previous two.
1904	175	1,100	Light, easy, fine.
1906-1910		Five-year contract at FF1,650	
1906	145		Complete, ripe tannins, no heaviness.
1907	165		Good wine, but not a great one. Quite light
1908	137		Chaptalised, robust and fruity.
1909	90		Harvest on 10 October. Chaptalised, average concentration, gracious.
1910	75		Chaptalised. Very little wine (mildew). (End of contract.)
1911	90	3,000	Concentrated and melting. A beautiful wine.
1912	145	1,850	A gentle, balanced wine, a little too liquid.
1913	125	2,300	Similar to 1912, but with a little more volume.
1914	95	2,200	A great classic wine.
1915	38		Disastrous wine which was not even sold (mildew).
1916	110	2,200 to 2,650	Harvest on 23 September. Powerful, strong, robust. Good wine.
1917-1921		Five-year contract at FF2,650	
1917	120		Rich, full-bodied, melting wine.
1918	160		Healthy, not too heavy, good.
1919	165		Smooth and elegant.
1920	125		Superb, rich, complete, good keeping qualities.
1921	140		Similar to the previous one, almost as perfect. (End of contract.)
1922	175	3,000 to 4,000	Lack of concentration, light.
1923	78	3,000 to 4,000	Sold to the firm Nicolas. Average, fragile wine.
1924	110	8,000	Sold to the firm of Félix Potin. A good rich wine with good keeping qualities.

Year	Number of Casks	Price per Cask in FF	Comment
1925	140	10,000	Rainy, October harvest. Watery, uninteresting wine.
1926	35	30,000	The opposite of 1925: concentrated, rich, good keeping qualities. Great wine.
1927	50	10,000	Insufficient maturity. Light, some charm.
1928	85	20,000	Great, very tannic wine. Good keeping qualities. For drinking in 2000, when it will be at its best.
1929	75	20,000	Great, supple, smooth, rich. Superb wine which has not reached its best yet.
1930	65		Mildew and rot. A very little wine.
1931	79		Sold in cases by Latour, but buyers could not be found. As mediocre as in 1930. Acid and chaptalised.
1932	90		Majority of the harvest (late October) declassified. Light, acid, uninteresting wine.
1933	65	11,500	This and previous year called "honest" wines.
1934	100	10,000 to 14,000	Well-balanced. Tannic, rich, good keeping qualities.
1935-1939		Contract with La Chevalerie.	
1935	94	12,800	Supple, thin, rather elegant.
1936	42	15,000	Thin, similar to the previous one.
1937	65	15,000	Tannic, concentrated, strong, austere. Similar to 1926, but not as good.
1938	75	25,000	Chaptalised, washed out and acid, fragile.
1939	100	20,000	Chaptalised, washed out and acid, fragile.
1940	67	25,000	Quite full, solid.
1941	85	130,000	Black market price. Light and balanced.
1942	65	130,000	Black market price. Concentrated, simple.
1943	75	100,000	Price fixed by decree. Strong and concentrated.
1944	91	100,000	Strong and light. Sold outside the fixed price: FF225,000.
1945	54	250,000	Very great tannic wine, powerful harmonious, good keeping qualities.
1946	50	140,000	Full-bodied, with "nerve".
1947	80	340,000 to 500,000	Powerful, rich, excessive, great.
1948	110	220,000	Tannins not ripe enough but powerful.
1949	110	300,000 to 400,000	Great simple wine, complete, rich, good keeping qualities.
1950	150	270,000 to 325,000	Good wine with ripe tannins.
1951	113	275,000	Chaptalised, acid, washed out, uninteresting. Overpriced.
1952	132	300,000	Rainy September harvest. Unripe tannins and acidity.
1953	190	400,000	Full, vinous, a touch of hardness. Similar to 1934 but stronger.
1954	105	300,000	Hard and little wine.
1955	170	700,000	Great wine similar to 1949, less powerful, more elegant.
1956	80	400,000	Year spoiled by frost. Light, rather acid wine.

Year	Number of Casks	Price per Cask in FF	Comment
1957	79	750,000 to 900,000	Insufficient maturity. Green tannins, acidity. Overpriced.
1958	118	525,000	Strong, average wine.
1959	118	1,000,000	Abundant, ripe tannins. A rich and balanced great wine.
1960	156	10,000 new francs *	Strong without body, a little wine.
1961	63	20,000	The greatest post-war Latour. Perfect, concentrated, very long keeping qualities. Reaching its best.
1962	125	12,000 to 15,000	Excellent, powerful and firm wine.
1963	150	20,000	Poor and acid. Very overpriced.
1963		Sale of Latour: new management, new technical team.	
1964	153 (total harvest: 200)	21,000	Exceptionally, Latour harvests early on 26 September (rain begins on the 27th). Balanced and lively.
1965	200	12,000	Acid (7 gr/l). 9°, chaptalised, thin.
1966	185	24,000 to 28,000	Great tannic wine, voluminous, good keeping qualities.
1967	142	19,000	Average body, limited maturity, poor keeping qualities.
1968	200	18,000	Green tannins, thin, uninteresting.
1969	75	48,000	Thin, light, acid. Overpriced.
1970	220 (total harvest: 417)	40,000 to 65,000	Powerful, despite an abundant harvest. Full, good keeping qualities.
1971	200	120,000	A little, firmer version of 1970. Exorbitant price.
1972	130 (total harvest: 288)	90,000	A little, dry, acid wine. Ridiculous price.
1973	225 (total harvest: 419)	25,000	Light, unconcentrated, easy, poor keeping qualities. Superabundant harvest.
1974	137	25,000	Too tannic (dry) for the small, weak body. Uninteresting.

* In 1960 the *"ancien"* franc becomes the *"nouveau"* franc. 100 old francs = 1 new franc

Year	No. of Latour Casks	No. of Forts de Latour Casks	Price per Cask in FF	Comment
1975	121	96	45,000	Very tannic, hard and fruity. Difficult to ascertain.
1976	191	124	50,000	Supple, unconcentrated.
1977	168	79	60,000	Neither concentrated nor full-bodied. A "light-weight".
1978	126	77	90,000	Tannic with volume. A good wine.
1979	218	138	90,000	Another late harvest, saved by modern agricultural methods. A very tannic wine, not yet fully balanced.
1980	101	65	90,000	Tannic, thin. Limited future.
1981	157	85	170,000	Tannic with acidity. A good but not great wine.
1982	175	79	230,000	Magnificently tannic and full. A great wine, more powerful than subtle. Highly characteristic in a "southern" style.

Year	Latour Casks	Forts de Latour Casks	Pauillac Casks	Hl/ha	Price per bottle of Latour in FF	Dates of Harvests	Comment
1983	274	154	none	70	170	22 Sept.-10 Oct.	Well constructed, average keeping qualities.
1984	184	86	none	45.2	180	1-14 Oct.	Green tannins and a certain acidic sharpness.
1985	240	104	none	61.6	210	30 Sept.-11 Oct.	Classic, balanced, complete and not showy, a great wine.
1986	224	104	none	55.9	180-210	30 Sept.-16 Oct.	Tannic wine, good keeping qualities, quite lively.
1987	190	88	32	49	130	30 Sept.-17 Oct.	An improved 1984, but thin and fragile.
1988	191	102	none	55.8	180	29 Sept.-10 Oct.	Well-built, balanced, virile, tannic, long-keeping.
1989	189	119	2	55.2	230-275	6-21 Sept.	A supple and more fruity 1988, ripe tannins.
1990	173	118	38	59.8	205-240	12 Sept.-2 Oct.	Like 1986, 1988 and 1989. Sumptuous tannins, a great wine.
1991	114	71	6	32.6	160	24 Sept.-10 Oct.	Rich for the year, well made.
1992	176	123	29	55.6	140	23 Sept.-9 Oct.	Supple, good for a poor year.
1993	237	152	14	68.3	155	22 Sept.-6 Oct.	Well-formed, full-bodied, suprising in view of a big harvest.
1994	188	128	34	58.9	180	13-29 Sept.	An average vintage, but extremely good results for Latour.
1995	187	106	21	50.6	250	13-27 Sept.	Excellent tannic wine with depth.
1996	183	120	20	53.3	400	17 Sept.-2 Oct.	Classic, harmonious, a long, great wine.
1997	187	164	29	60	500	8-25 Sept.	Only slightly inferior to 1995.

N.B. In the above tables, the comments given are relative to a *grand cru classé*; a "poor" or "little" wine for a *grand cru* remains a great wine.

CHATEAU LA̶TOUR

CONCLUSION

f tradition is to be believed, those who own historic monuments or great works of art are more the servants of their possessions than the masters. They have a moral – sometimes even a legal – obligation to perpetuate and transmit. The same applies to the greatest French wines, the *premiers crus*.

It is suprising that no comparative history of the *premiers crus* has ever been published. A study of Latour indicates that these exceptional wines have much in common. They are both brothers and competitors; they were born in the same era, grew up together and fought the same fights. This similarity has given rise to competition but also to emulation. Each has tried to produce the best wine, the one which would sell for the highest price. The contract system which wholesale wine merchants proposed to all of the producers in the last century did something to remove competition between them. In the same way, the three terrible diseases which attacked them in the nineteenth century contributed to a closer working relationship between the wine producers. They applied the same remedies, and yields per hectare increased simultaneously.

Conversely, the collapse in the price of wine at the end of the nineteenth century inspired an identical strategy of reduction in yield. One can thus validly ponder the question of how much room for manœuvre a wine-producer really has, even for a *grand cru*. He cannot ignore market forces but needs to find out whether the market is active or reactive.

There are two situations which need to be distinguished from each other: the consequences of underconsumption, and the problems posed by under-production.

For several centuries the *premiers crus* have been the world reference point. This continuity is all the more remarkable when we look at the way the wine has evolved over the past two hundred and fifty years. The 1730 Latour, product of a vineyard planted mainly with Malbec, produced the equivalent of 10 hectolitres per hectare. This wine is not quite the same as the 1800 vintage, when the vineyard was producing nearly 16 hl/ha, nor yet that which preceded the "golden age" (13 hl/ha). The difference is even more marked in the case of the famous golden-age wine (nearly 19 hl/ha with different vine stocks, inlcuding some Merlot). All these successive wines bear little resemblance to today's Château Latour, whose dynamic vineyard is capable of producing between 40 and 55 hl/ha (the most productive, young vines are in the Forts de Latour).

In 1895, the Marquis de Flers wrote: "My express opinion is not to sacrifice quality in order to improve the quantity of the product." The regular increase in yield of the *grands crus* obviously poses the question of the limit beyond which quality is liable to be sacrificed. A good basis for discussion could be the conclusion shared by all connoisseurs of Château Latour — that the greatest wine produced by the estate in the last fifty years is indisputably the 1961 vintage.

GRAPE HARVESTER CARRYING HIS LOAD

FAMILY PORTRAITS

FRANÇOIS PINAULT

THE MEN & WOMEN

of

CHÂTEAU LATOUR

WINERY MASTER

VINE-GROWER

GRAPE-PICKER

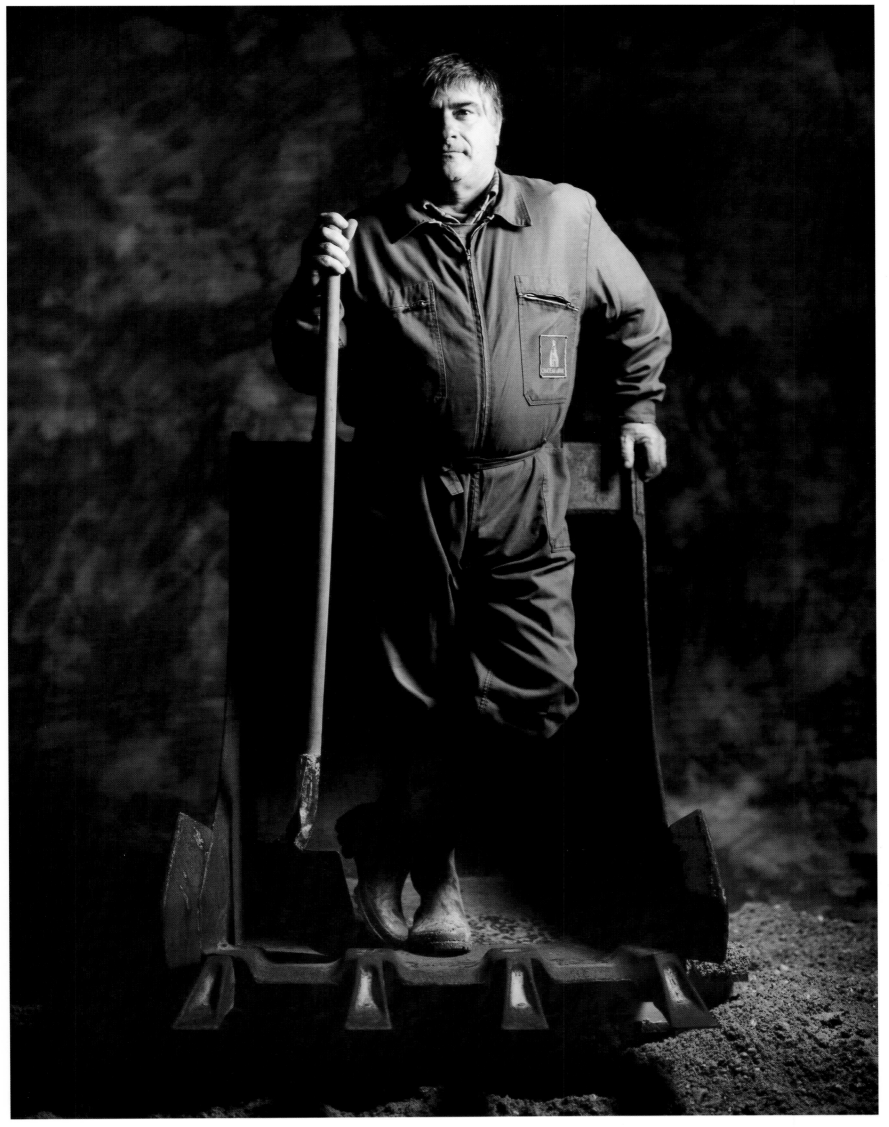

MAINTENANCE MAN

THE HEAD GROWER

THE COOKS *hired at harvest time*

MAINTENANCE MAN

THE SECRETARY

GENERAL STATISTICS

Total area	**99.1 hectares**		
Vineyard area	**65.4 hectares**	*Petit Batailley*	*11.8 hectares*
"The Enclosure"	*46.9 hectares*	*Comtesse*	*2.7 hectares*
External plots of land	*18.5 hectares*	*Sainte Anne*	*4.0 hectares*

Vine stocks	**Grand Vin**	**Forts Latour**
Cabernet Sauvignon	*75%*	*65%*
Merlot	*20%*	*35%*
Cabernet Franc & Petit Verdot	*5%*	

Grafting stocks	*Riparia Gloire*
	101-14 & 3309 C
	some SO4 (Batailley)

Average production	**3300 hl/hectare**		
at the time of putting down	*Chateau Latour*	*220,000 bottles*	*56%*
	Forts de Latour	*140,000 bottles*	*36%*
	Pauillac	*30,000 bottles*	*8%*
	Total	**390,000 bottles**	

Storage in vats

14 x 205 hl vats (1964)	*2870 hl*	
5 x 145 hl vats (1970)	*725 hl*	**5550 hl**
8 x 179 hl vats (1989)	*1430 hl*	
5 x 105 hl vats (1991)	*525 hl*	

Storage in the wine store

1st year	*in the ground*	*950 casks*
	maille perdue	*1400 casks*
	maille pleine	*1850 casks*
2nd year	*in other*	*1450 casks*

The team

Owner/Manager: *François Pinault (since 1993)*
Estate manager: *Christian Le Sommer (since 1986)*
Sales manager: *Frédéric Engerer (since 1995)*
Farm manager: *Frédéric Ardouin (since 1996)*
Winery master: *Denis Malbec (since 1994)*

THE LORDS OF LATOUR

THE CO-SEIGNEURS (only the most important are listed)

Years	Family names
1330-1360	de Castillon
1350-1450	Albret
1350-1450	Montferrand
1340-1595	Saint-Genès
1390-1450	la Motte
1390-1450	Treulo, Makanam
1460-1571	de l'Isle

THE LORDS OF LATOUR

de Mullet family
- 1595-1607 Arnaud de Mullet (through purchase)
- 1607-1656 Denis I de Mullet
- 1656-1660 Denis II de Mullet (a minor, his mother Jeanne ran the estate)
- 1660-1670 Catherine Daulède, née de Mullet (daughter of Denis I), with her son Jean-Denis Daulède

The Chanevas/de Ségur heirs:

29 June 1670 ?	François Chanevas (acquisition)
?-1693	Marguerite Coutant (niece of Chanevas)
1693-1716	Marie-Thérèse de Clausel (daughter of Mme Coutant, married Alexandre de Ségur in 1695)
1716-1755	Nicolas-Alexandre de Ségur
1755-1761/63	Alexandre de Ségur

from 1761-63 Comtesse de Maisoncel / Comtesse de Miromesnil / Comtesse de Coëtlogon } undivided ownership between the daughters of Nicolas-Alexandre

1786-1796 Comte de Ségur-Cabanac (partial inheritance from Mme Maisoncel and Mme Coëtlogon)

The last Lords of Latour and their shares:
Comte de Ségur-Cabanac (27.06%)
Vicomtesse de la Pallu (36.47%) } daughters of the Comtesse de Miromesnil
Marquise de Beaumont (36.47%)

– The French Revolution –

Owners of Latour

Vicomtesse de la Pallu
|
Marquis de Courtivron

Marquise de Beaumont
|
Marquis de Beaumont-Villenauzy   Marquise de Flers
Comte Léon de Beaumont   Marquis de Fayet

Owners of the *quart Latour* between 1796 and 1841

MONTBALON	MME CORRÉGEOLES-TEULON	MME CORREGEOLES-CLAMAGERAN
1839	Pierre Bosc	Year V Labarrère
P. F. Guestier	1840 N. Johnston	Year X Conte
N. Johnston		1833 P. F. Guestier-N. Barton
The Ségur heirs		

1841

Auction sale of the Latour Estate
Acquisition of the estate by the Ségur heirs:
Beaumont, Beaumont-Villemauzy, Courtivron, Fayet and de Flers

1842

Foundation of the *Société civile du vignoble de Latour* (% of shares rounded up)

Shareholders: Marquis de Courtivron (24.3%)
Marquis de Flers (23.6%)
Marquis de Beaumont-Villemauzy (17.4%)
Marquis de Fayet (17.4%)
Comte Léon de Beaumont (17.4%)

1963

New shareholders:
Hallminster Ltd. (Pearson Group) (53%)
Harveys (25%)
The Ségur (Beaumont) heirs (22%)

1989

New shareholders:
Allied-Lyons (93.2%)
Miscellaneous (6.8%)

1993

New shareholders:
Artémis (François Pinault)
Miscellaneous owners (6.8%)

PRICE PER BOTTLE

OF NEW WINE SINCE 1945

Average price where selling price was not uniform
(in French francs at their 1997 value)

1945	142	1972	387
1946	652	1973	98
1947	105	1974	86
1948	35	1975	139
1949	49	1976	140
1950	37	1977	155
1951	30	1978	213
1952	29	1979	192
1953	39	1980	170
1954	30	1981	285
1955	68	1982	342
1956	37	1983	259
1957	75	1984	255
1958	42	1985	282
1959	75	1986	274
1960	78	1987	165
1961	139	1988	222
1962	89	1989	297
1963	126	1990	259
1964	128	1991	179
1965	65	1992	153
1966	150	1993	165
1967	107	1994	189
1968	97	1995	258
1969	245	1996	405
1970	253	1997	500
1971	549		

ACKNOWLEDGEMENTS

The publisher and author would like to thank the team at Château Latour
for their help in producing this book. In particular, they wish to express their gratitude to
François Pinault for opening up the estate to them,
Jean-Louis Deroux, who spared so much of his valuable time
and Frédéric Engerer, for his invaluable advice.

The author relied on two main sources for his research, the Château Latour archives and the compilation *La Seigneurie et le vignoble de Château Latour* (Fédération historique du Sud-Ouest, Bordeaux, 1974).